1 Longman Academic Reading Series

READING SKILLS FOR COLLEGE

Elizabeth Böttcher

Dedication

To my mother, Suzy Schwartz, whose love and light continue to support and guide me, and to my mother-in-law, Rosamarie Böttcher, for her love and encouragement.

Elizabeth Böttcher

Longman Academic Reading Series 1: Reading Skills for College

Pearson Education, 10 Bank Street, White Plains, NY 10606

Staff Credits: The people who made up the **Longman Academic Reading Series 1** team, representing editorial, production, design, and manufacturing, are Pietro Alongi, Margaret Antonini, Rosa Chapinal, Aerin Csigay, Ann France, Françoise Leffler, Amy McCormick, Liza Pleva, Mary Perrotta Rich, Massimo Rubini, and Robert Ruvo.

Cover image: The Loupe Project/Shutterstock
Text Composition: TSI Graphics

Library of Congress Cataloging-in-Publication Data
  Böttcher, Elizabeth.
   Longman Academic Reading Series / Elizabeth Bottcher.
     volumes cm
   Includes index.
   ISBN 978-0-13-278664-5 (Level 1)—ISBN 978-0-13-278582-2 (Level 2)—
  ISBN 978-0-13-276059-1 (Level 3)—ISBN 978-0-13-276061-4 (Level 4)—
  ISBN 978-0-13-276067-6 (Level 5)
   1. English language—Textbooks for foreign speakers. 2. Reading comprehension—Problems, exercises, etc. 3. College readers. I. Title.
   PE1128.B637 2013
   428.6'4—dc23

                         2013007701

ISBN 10: 0-13-278664-8
ISBN 13: 978-0-13-278664-5

Printed in the United States of America
1 2 3 4 5 6 7 8 9 10—V082—18 17 16 15 14 13

CONTENTS

TO THE TEACHER

Welcome to the *Longman Academic Reading Series,* a five-level series that prepares English-language learners for academic work. The aim of the series is to make students more effective and confident readers by providing **high-interest readings on academic subjects** and teaching them **skills and strategies** for

- effective reading
- vocabulary building
- note-taking
- critical thinking

Last but not least, the series encourages students to **discuss and write** about the ideas they have discovered in the readings, making them better speakers and writers of English as well.

High-Interest Readings On Academic Subjects

Research shows that if students are not motivated to read, if reading is not in some sense enjoyable, the reading process becomes mechanical drudgery and the potential for improvement is minimal. That is why high-interest readings are the main feature in the *Longman Academic Reading Series.*

Varied High-Interest Texts

Each chapter of each book in the series focuses on an engaging theme from a wide range of academic subjects, such as art, health sciences, animal behavior, and government. The reading selections in each chapter (two readings in Level 1 and three in Levels 2–5) are chosen to provide different and intriguing perspectives on the theme. These readings come from a variety of sources or genres—books, textbooks, transcripts, newspapers, magazines, online articles—and are written by a variety of authors from widely different fields. The Level 1 book, for instance, offers a short biography of Sonia Sotomayor, a book review of *Who Moved My Cheese?*, a history of the Navajo Code Talkers, and a description of the life-altering Blue Eyes-Brown Eyes lesson—all challenging reading selections that spark students' interest and motivate them to read and discuss what they read.

Academic Work

The work done in response to these selections provides students with a reading and discussion experience that mirrors the in-depth treatment of texts in academic course work. Although the readings may be adapted for the lower levels and excerpted for the upper levels, the authentic reading experience has been preserved. The series sustains students' interest and gives a sample of the types of content and reasoning that are the hallmark of academic work.

Skills and Strategies

To help students read and understand its challenging readings, the *Longman Academic Reading Series* provides a battery of skills and strategies for effective reading, vocabulary building, note-taking, and critical thinking.

Effective Reading

The series provides students with strategies that will help them learn to skim, scan, predict, preview, map, and formulate questions before they begin to read. After they read, students are routinely asked to identify main ideas as well as supporting details. Students using this series learn to uncover what is beneath the surface of a reading passage and are led to interpret the many layers of meaning in a text. Each text is an invitation to dig deeper.

Vocabulary Building

In all chapters students are given the opportunity to see and use vocabulary in many ways: guessing words in context (an essential skill, without which fluent reading is impossible), identifying synonyms and antonyms, recognizing idioms, practicing word forms, as well as using new words in their own spoken and written sentences. At the same time, students learn the best strategies for using the dictionary effectively, and have ample practice in recognizing collocations, understanding connotations, and communicating in the discourse specific to certain disciplines. The intentional "recycling" of vocabulary in both speaking and writing activities provides students with an opportunity to use the vocabulary they have acquired.

Note-Taking

As students learn ways to increase their reading comprehension and their retention of main ideas and details, they are encouraged to practice and master a variety of note-taking skills, such as underlining, annotating, sorting, summarizing, and outlining. The skills that form the focus of each chapter have been systematically aligned with the skills practiced in other chapters, so that scaffolding improves overall reading competence within each level.

Critical Thinking

At all levels of proficiency, students become more skilled in the process of analysis as they learn to read between the lines, make inferences, draw conclusions, make connections, evaluate, and synthesize information from various sources. The aim of this reflective journey is the development of students' critical thinking ability, which is achieved in different ways in each chapter.

Speaking and Writing

The speaking activities that frame and contribute to the development of each chapter tap students' strengths, allow them to synthesize information from several sources, and give them a sense of community in the reading experience. In addition, because good readers make good writers, students are given the opportunity to express themselves in a writing activity in each chapter.

The aim of the *Longman Academic Reading Series* is to provide "teachable" books that allow instructors to recognize the flow of ideas in each lesson and to choose from many types of exercises to get the students interested and to maintain their active participation throughout. By showing students how to appreciate the ideas that make the readings memorable, the series encourages students to become more effective, confident, and independent readers.

The Online Teacher's Manual

The Teacher's Manual is available at www.pearsonelt.com/tmkeys. It includes general teaching notes, chapter teaching notes, answer keys, and reproducible chapter quizzes.

CHAPTER OVERVIEW

All chapters in the *Longman Academic Reading Series, Level 1*
have the same basic structure.

Objectives

BEFORE YOU READ

Consider These Questions/Facts/Chart/etc.

READING ONE: [+ *reading title*]

A. Warm-Up

B. Reading Strategy

[Reading One]

COMPREHENSION

A. Main Ideas

B. Close Reading

VOCABULARY *[not necessarily in this order; other activities possible]*

A. Definitions

B. Synonyms

C. Using the Dictionary

D. Parts of Speech

CRITICAL THINKING

READING TWO: [+ *reading title*]

A. Warm-Up

B. Reading Strategy

[Reading Two]

COMPREHENSION

A. Main Ideas

B. Close Reading

VOCABULARY *[not necessarily in this order; other activities also possible]*

A. Guessing from Context

B. Prefixes

C. Collocations

D. Word Forms

NOTE-TAKING *[only one per chapter; in either reading section]*

CRITICAL THINKING

AFTER YOU READ

WRITING ACTIVITY

DISCUSSION AND WRITING TOPICS

Vocabulary
Self-Assessment

Each chapter starts with a definition of the chapter's academic subject matter, Objectives, and a Before You Read section.

A short **definition of the academic subject** mentioned in the chapter title describes the general area of knowledge explored in the chapter.

Chapter objectives provide clear goals for students by listing the skills they will practice in the chapter.

Each of the two reading sections in a chapter starts with a Warm-Up activity and a Reading Strategy presentation and practice, followed by the reading itself.

The **Before You Read** activities introduce the subject matter of the chapter, using a mix of information and questions to stimulate students' interest.

BEFORE YOU READ

Consider These Questions

Discuss the questions in a small group.

1. What kind of animal makes the best pet?
2. Why do you think this animal is a good pet?

READING ONE: In the Presence of Animals

A Warm-Up

Check (✓) the statements you think are true about dogs.

☐ 1. They help people who are sick get better.
☐ 2. They make people feel relaxed.
☐ 3. They are good listeners.
☐ 4. They are good pets for people of all ages.

The **Warm-Up** activity presents discussion questions that activate students' prior knowledge and help them develop a personal connection with the topic of the reading.

B Reading Strategy

Predicting Content Using Visuals

Predicting is a very important pre-reading skill. When you **predict**, you make a guess about something based on the information you have. Predicting helps prepare the reader for the reading experience that is to come. Pictures in a text can often help you predict what the text is about.

Look at the picture in the reading. What do you think is going on? Circle one of the choices and discuss your answer with a partner.

   a. a dog gets sick and goes to the hospital
   b. a dog visits a sick person in the hospital
   c. a dog cannot be separated from his owner

Now read the text to find out if your prediction was correct.

The **Reading Strategy** box gives a general description of a reading strategy, such as predicting content using visuals, and the reasons for using it. The **activities** below the box show students how to apply that strategy to the reading.

Reading One sets the theme and presents the basic ideas that will be explored in the chapter. Like all the readings in the series, it is an example of a genre of writing (here, a magazine article).

In the Presence of Animals

By Sarah Burke in *Science and Society*

1   As far back as the 1790s, the owners of a senior citizens' home in York, England, encouraged patients to spend time with farm animals, believing that this would help their mental state[1] more than the sometimes harsh therapies[2] used on the mentally ill at the time. In recent years, scientists have finally begun to find proof that contact with animals can increase a sick person's chance of survival and has been shown to lower heart rate, calm upset children, and get people to start a conversation.

2   Scientists think that animal companionship[3] is beneficial because animals are accepting and attentive,[4] and they don't criticize or give orders. Animals also have a unique ability to get people to be more social. Visitors to nursing homes, for example, get more social responses from patients when they come with animal companions, researchers have found.

3   Not only do people seem happier when animals are nearby, but they may also live longer. Studies show that a year after heart surgery, survival rates for heart patients were higher for those with pets in their homes than those without pets. Elderly people with pets make fewer trips to doctors than those who are without animal companions, possibly because animals lessen loneliness. A professor of public health at UCLA says that pet ownership might provide a new form of "low-cost health intervention."[5]

[1] *mental state:* emotional condition
[2] *therapies:* treatments
[3] *companionship:* friendship
[4] *accepting and attentive:* agreeable and caring

[5] *intervention:* the act of preventing something undesirable (unwanted)

READING TWO: Canine Companions May Help Kids Learn to Read

A Warm-Up

Read the quotation. Check (✓) the sentences that have the same meaning as the quote.

"An animal's eyes have the power to speak a great language."

—*Martin Buber, philosopher*

☐ **1.** Animals communicate a lot of feelings with their eyes.

☐ **2.** Animals use their eyes to speak to us.

☐ **3.** When animals look at us, we feel connected to them.

B Reading Strategy

Predicting Content from the Title

Predicting is a very important pre-reading skill. When you **predict**, you make a guess about something based on the information you have. Predicting helps prepare the reader for the reading experience that is to come. The title of a text can often help you predict what the text is about.

The title of the reading is "Canine Companions May Help Kids Learn to Read." With a partner, write two predictions about the content of the reading.

1. _____

2. _____

Now read the article to find out if your predictions were correct.

Health Sciences: *The Therapeutic Effects of Animals* **7**

Reading Two addresses the same theme as Reading One, but from a completely different perspective. In most cases, it is also an example of a different genre of writing (here, an online article).

All readings have **numbered paragraphs** for easy reference. The **target vocabulary** that students need to know in order to read academic texts is set in boldface blue for easy recognition. Target vocabulary is recycled through the chapter and the level.

Most readings have **glosses** and **footnotes** to help students understand difficult words and names.

Canine Companions May Help Kids Learn to Read
By Maryann Mott for *National Geographic News*

Walk into a Salt Lake City public library on a Saturday afternoon and you might see something you didn't expect: children reading books to dogs. Three years ago, Intermountain Therapy Animals (ITA) started the R.E.A.D.® (Reading Education Assistance Dogs) program at the suggestion of board member Sandi Martin, a nurse and a long-time supporter of pets in hospitals, who had seen the positive effect animals can have on mentally and physically challenged[1] children. If therapy dogs help those children, thought Martin, who loves to read, then perhaps they can help kids who are struggling with reading, too.

2 The program is simple. For about 30 minutes each week, kids from five to nine years old read aloud to dogs of all shapes and sizes. The people in charge of the dogs sit nearby to help. Martin says children are more willing to read to dogs than to their classmates, in part because kids who stumble over[2] new words know their furry friends won't make fun of them. As a result, children's reading skills improve and their self-esteem grows.

[1] *mentally or physically challenged:* having a more difficult time with mental or physical skills than the average person

[2] *stumble over:* to have difficulty doing something; hesitate

8 CHAPTER 1

Each reading in the chapter is followed by Comprehension and Vocabulary activities.

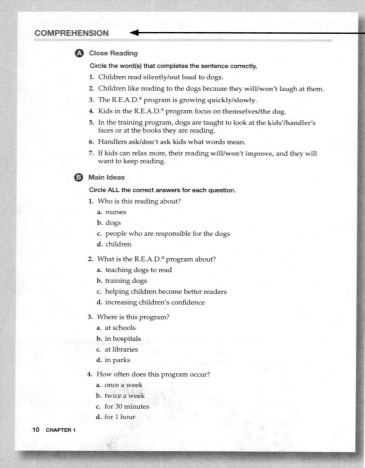

COMPREHENSION

A Close Reading

Circle the word(s) that completes the sentence correctly.

1. Children read silently/out loud to dogs.
2. Children like reading to the dogs because they will/won't laugh at them.
3. The R.E.A.D.® program is growing quickly/slowly.
4. Kids in the R.E.A.D.® program focus on themselves/the dog.
5. In the training program, dogs are taught to look at the kids'/handler's faces or at the books they are reading.
6. Handlers ask/don't ask kids what words mean.
7. If kids can relax more, their reading will/won't improve, and they will want to keep reading.

B Main Ideas

Circle ALL the correct answers for each question.

1. Who is this reading about?
   a. nurses
   b. dogs
   c. people who are responsible for the dogs
   d. children

2. What is the R.E.A.D.® program about?
   a. teaching dogs to read
   b. training dogs
   c. helping children become better readers
   d. increasing children's confidence

3. Where is this program?
   a. at schools
   b. in hospitals
   c. at libraries
   d. in parks

4. How often does this program occur?
   a. once a week
   b. twice a week
   c. for 30 minutes
   d. for 1 hour

10   CHAPTER 1

The **Comprehension** activities help students identify and understand the main ideas of the reading and their supporting details.

The **Vocabulary** activities focus on the target vocabulary in the reading, presenting and practicing skills such as guessing meaning from context or from synonyms, using a dictionary, and understanding word usage.

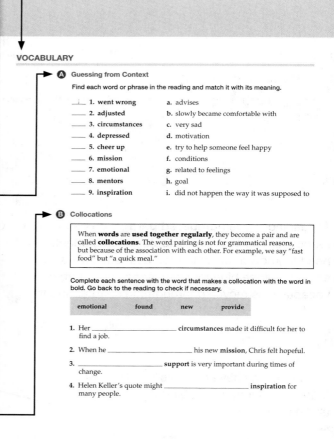

VOCABULARY

A Guessing from Context

Find each word or phrase in the reading and match it with its meaning.

___i___ 1. went wrong	a. advises
_____ 2. adjusted	b. slowly became comfortable with
_____ 3. circumstances	c. very sad
_____ 4. depressed	d. motivation
_____ 5. cheer up	e. try to help someone feel happy
_____ 6. mission	f. conditions
_____ 7. emotional	g. related to feelings
_____ 8. mentors	h. goal
_____ 9. inspiration	i. did not happen the way it was supposed to

B Collocations

When **words** are **used together regularly**, they become a pair and are called **collocations**. The word pairing is not for grammatical reasons, but because of the association with each other. For example, we say "fast food" but "a quick meal."

Complete each sentence with the word that makes a collocation with the word in bold. Go back to the reading to check if necessary.

emotional	found	new	provide

1. Her _____ **circumstances** made it difficult for her to find a job.
2. When he _____ his new **mission**, Chris felt hopeful.
3. _____ **support** is very important during times of change.
4. Helen Keller's quote might _____ **inspiration** for many people.

20   CHAPTER 2

The **Guessing from Context** activity helps students guess the meaning of the target vocabulary by encouraging them to go back to the reading to find clues in the context, and then base their guesses on these clues.

The **Collocation** activity helps students understand how words go together in English. Students are encouraged to go back to the reading to find the vocabulary words and the words they are regularly used with.

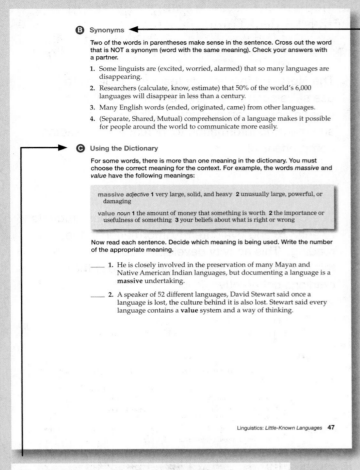

B Synonyms

Two of the words in parentheses make sense in the sentence. Cross out the word that is NOT a synonym (word with the same meaning). Check your answers with a partner.

1. Some linguists are (excited, worried, alarmed) that so many languages are disappearing.

2. Researchers (calculate, know, estimate) that 50% of the world's 6,000 languages will disappear in less than a century.

3. Many English words (ended, originated, came) from other languages.

4. (Separate, Shared, Mutual) comprehension of a language makes it possible for people around the world to communicate more easily.

C Using the Dictionary

For some words, there is more than one meaning in the dictionary. You must choose the correct meaning for the context. For example, the words *massive* and *value* have the following meanings:

> **massive** *adjective* **1** very large, solid, and heavy **2** unusually large, powerful, or damaging
>
> **value** *noun* **1** the amount of money that something is worth **2** the importance or usefulness of something **3** your beliefs about what is right or wrong

Now read each sentence. Decide which meaning is being used. Write the number of the appropriate meaning.

_____ 1. He is closely involved in the preservation of many Mayan and Native American Indian languages, but documenting a language is a **massive** undertaking.

_____ 2. A speaker of 52 different languages, David Stewart said once a language is lost, the culture behind it is also lost. Stewart said every language contains a **value** system and a way of thinking.

Linguistics: *Little-Known Languages* **47**

The **Synonyms** activity also helps students understand the meaning of the target vocabulary in the reading, but here for each target word students are given synonyms to match or choose from.

The **Word Usage** activity shows students some of the ways English speakers use a word or idiom featured in the reading, and then checks students' understanding.

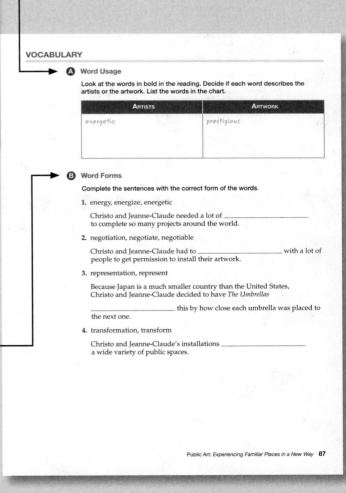

VOCABULARY

A Word Usage

Look at the words in bold in the reading. Decide if each word describes the artists or the artwork. List the words in the chart.

Artists	Artwork
energetic	prestigious

B Word Forms

Complete the sentences with the correct form of the words.

1. energy, energize, energetic

   Christo and Jeanne-Claude needed a lot of _____ to complete so many projects around the world.

2. negotiation, negotiate, negotiable

   Christo and Jeanne-Claude had to _____ with a lot of people to get permission to install their artwork.

3. representation, represent

   Because Japan is a much smaller country than the United States, Christo and Jeanne-Claude decided to have *The Umbrellas*

   _____ this by how close each umbrella was placed to the next one.

4. transformation, transform

   Christo and Jeanne-Claude's installations _____ a wide variety of public spaces.

Public Art: *Experiencing Familiar Places in a New Way* **87**

The **Using the Dictionary** activity shows students how to understand a dictionary entry. Students choose the appropriate meaning of the word as it is used in the reading and in other contexts.

The **Word Forms** activity helps students expand their vocabulary by encouraging them to guess or find out the different forms some of the target words can have. Then students are challenged to use the forms correctly.

One of the two reading sections in a chapter has a Note-Taking activity. Both reading sections end with a Critical Thinking activity.

NOTE-TAKING: Writing Margin Notes

Writing notes in the margins will help you keep track of the important ideas in a text. Use the *wh-* questions to decide what is most important in the paragraph.

Write notes in the margin next to the paragraphs from the reading. The first paragraph is done as an example. Use the *wh-* words as a guide.

In most Hollywood movies, the Native American Navajos still fight on horses in the American Southwest. But during World War II, a group of Navajos made their language into a weapon to protect the United States. They were the Navajo Code Talkers, and theirs is one of the few unbroken codes in military history.

WHAT?
Navajos, not only in movies
Navajo language, weapon in WW II
unbroken military code

Navajo was the perfect choice for a secret language. It is very **complex**. One vowel can have up to 10 different pronunciations, changing the meaning of any word. In the 1940s, Navajo was an unwritten language. No one outside of the reservation could speak it or understand it.

WHY?

The Navajo Code team had to invent new words to describe military equipment. For example, they named ships after fish: *lotso-whale* (battleship), *calo-shark* (destroyer), and *beshloiron-fish* (submarine). When a Code Talker received a message via radio, he heard a series of unrelated Navajo words. He would then translate the words into English and use the first letter of each English word to spell the message. The Navajo words *tsah* (needle), *wol-la-chee* (ant), *ah-kh-di-glini* (victor), and *tsah-ah-dzoh* (yucca) spelled *NAVY*.

HOW?

40 CHAPTER 3

The **Note-Taking** activity teaches students to use skills such as circling, underlining, writing margin notes, categorizing, outlining, and summarizing information to increase their reading comprehension.

The **Critical Thinking** activity encourages students to analyze and evaluate the information in the reading. This activity develops students' critical thinking skills and their ability to express their opinions coherently.

CRITICAL THINKING

Discuss the questions with a partner. Be prepared to share your ideas with the class.

1. President Obama said that Sonia Sotomayor's journey symbolizes the American dream. What do you think this means?
2. What qualities and qualifications does Sotomayor have that make her a valuable Supreme Court justice?
3. If you could meet Sotomayor, what questions would you want to ask her?
4. Do you find Sonia Sotomayor's life story inspiring? Why or Why not?"

AFTER YOU READ

WRITING ACTIVITY

Choose one of the topics. Use at least five of the words and phrases you studied in the chapter (for a complete list, go to page 119).

1. If you were a member of Congress and were interviewing a potential Supreme Court justice, what questions would you ask? What would you want to know before you confirmed a candidate? Write three questions.
2. Read about the current Supreme Court justices. Write a paragraph about one of the justices you find interesting.

DISCUSSION AND WRITING TOPICS

Discuss these topics in a small group. Choose one of them and write a paragraph about it. Use the vocabulary from the chapter.

1. Should all judges be in their jobs for life? Why do you think some judges are elected and some are appointed?
2. Do you think it is a difficult job to be a Supreme Court justice? Why or why not?

118 CHAPTER 8

Each chapter ends with an After You Read section, a Vocabulary chart, and a Self-Assessment.

The **After You Read** activities go back to the theme of the chapter, encouraging students to discuss and write about related topics using the target vocabulary of the chapter.

AFTER YOU READ

WRITING ACTIVITY

Make a list of what you buy in a day or a week. Then write a paragraph answering the questions. Use at least five of the words and phrases you studied in the chapter (for a complete list, go to page 132).

- Is everything you buy a necessity?
- Are there items you could choose not to buy, and it would not affect your life?
- Which items would be easiest to give up?

DISCUSSION AND WRITING TOPICS

Discuss these topics in a small group. Choose one of them and write a paragraph or two about it. Use the vocabulary from the chapter.

1. Would you have agreed to be part of an experiment to live without money? Why or why not?

2. What do you think you would miss the most if you lived without money for a time?

Could you choose to not buy food and eat what grows naturally around you?

Economics: *Bartering in the 21st Century* **131**

The **Vocabulary chart**, which lists all the target vocabulary words of the chapter under the appropriate parts of speech, provides students with a convenient reference.

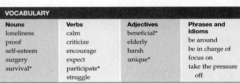

VOCABULARY

Nouns	Verbs	Adjectives	Phrases and Idioms
loneliness	calm	beneficial*	be around
proof	criticize	elderly	be in charge of
self-esteem	encourage	harsh	focus on
surgery	expect	unique*	take the pressure off
survival*	participate*		
	struggle		

* = AWL (Academic Word List) item

SELF-ASSESSMENT

In this chapter you learned to:

- ○ Preveiw and predict the content of a text using visuals
- ○ Preview and predict the content of a text from its title
- ○ Guess the meaning of words from the context
- ○ Determine whether a word has a positive or negative meaning
- ○ Identify word forms from location in the sentence
- ○ Use a dictionary to find noun forms of verbs
- ○ Use underlining to identify numbers and summarize a text

What can you do well? ⟲

What do you need to practice more? ⟲

The **Self-Assessment** checklist encourages students to evaluate their own progress. Have they mastered the skills listed in the chapter objectives?

Health Sciences: *The Therapeutic Effects of Animals* **15**

SCOPE AND SEQUENCE

CHAPTER	READING	VOCABULARY
1 HEALTH SCIENCES: The Therapeutic Effects of Animals **Theme:** How animals can help us **Reading One:** *In the Presence of Animals* (a magazine article) **Reading Two:** *Canine Companions May Help Kids Learn to Read* (an online article)	• Understand and practice different reading strategies • Predict the content of a text by using visuals • Predict the content of a text from its title • Identify the main ideas of a text • Understand the details that support the main ideas	• Guess the meaning of words from the context • Recognize and learn the connotations of words • Identify and use different word forms • Categorize words by part of speech • Use the Vocabulary list at the end of the chapter to review the words, phrases, and idioms learned in the chapter • Use this vocabulary in the After You Read speaking and writing activities
2 PSYCHOLOGY: Dealing with Change **Theme:** How to make the best of a changed situation **Reading One:** *Young Football Players Injured, but Not Forgotten* (a television news story) **Reading Two:** *Who Moved My Cheese?* (a book review)	• Understand and practice different reading strategies • Skim a text to find the main idea • Identify the type of text to prepare for the reading • Identify or complete the main ideas of a text • Understand the details that support the main ideas	• Guess the meaning of words from the context • Understand and use synonyms and collocations • Understand and sort words by part of speech • Use the Vocabulary list at the end of the chapter to review the words, phrases, and idioms learned in the chapter • Use this vocabulary in the After You Read speaking and writing activities
3 LINGUISTICS: Little-Known Languages **Theme:** The importance of languages and how they are used **Reading One:** *An Unbreakable Code* (a magazine article) **Reading Two:** *Languages Die Out, Taking History Along* (an online article)	• Understand and practice different reading strategies • Preview a text using visuals like charts or graphs • Scan a text to look for specific information • Understand the introduction of a text and how it is organized • Identify the main ideas of a text • Understand the details that support the main ideas	• Guess the meaning of words from the context • Use dictionary entries to choose the correct meaning of words for the context • Understand and use synonyms, prefixes, and suffixes • Use the Vocabulary list at the end of the chapter to review the words, phrases, and idioms learned in the chapter • Use this vocabulary in the After You Read speaking and writing activities

NOTE-TAKING	CRITICAL THINKING	SPEAKING/WRITING
• Use underlining to identify and remember important facts in a story	• Express opinions and support your opinions with examples from a text or from your own experience and culture • Analyze and evaluate information • Infer information not explicit in a text • Draw conclusions • Make connections between ideas • Synthesize information and ideas	• Describe a situation that you imagine • Discuss which animals might be used for therapeutic purposes • Discuss the benefits of having a pet • Choose one of the topics and write a paragraph or two about it
• Fill out an organizer using the answers to *wh-* questions to summarize a reading	• Answer questions based on information in a text or on your own experience and culture • Analyze and evaluate information • Infer information not explicit in a text • Draw conclusions about the moral of a parable • Make connections between ideas • Synthesize information and ideas	• Discuss the meaning of a photo and a quote • Write two paragraphs about a change you experienced • Discuss the topic of change and whether it is positive or negative • Choose one of the topics and write a paragraph or two about it
• Use margin notes to identify important facts in a reading • Use *wh-* questions to determine what is important in a reading	• Express opinions and support your opinions with examples from a text or from your own experience and culture • Analyze and evaluate information • Infer information not explicit in a text • Draw conclusions • Evaluate if an author presents both sides of a topic equally • Make connections between ideas	• Talk about the importance of languages and the benefits of speaking a language • Talk about codes and why they would be useful • Discuss how the values of a culture are expressed through its language • Choose one of the topics and write a paragraph or two about it

CHAPTER	READING	VOCABULARY
4 ANIMAL BEHAVIOR: Elephants **Theme:** The care of elephant orphans and how elephants are like humans **Reading One:** *The Elephant Orphanage* (a television documentary transcript) **Reading Two:** *Elephant Behavior* (an article)	• Understand and practice different reading strategies • Skim a reading to get an overview of its contents • Use key words and phrases in the topic sentence to help determine the main idea • Identify the main ideas of a text • Understand the details that support the main ideas	• Guess the meaning of words from the context • Understand and use synonyms and word forms • Categorize words by parts of speech • Use the Vocabulary list at the end of the chapter to review the words, phrases, and idioms learned in the chapter • Use this vocabulary in the After You Read speaking and writing activities
5 SOCIAL PSYCHOLOGY: Teaching Tolerance **Theme:** How the experience of discrimination affects people **Reading One:** *A Class Divided—Jane Elliott's Famous Lesson* (an online article) **Reading Two:** *Fourteen Years Later* (a television transcript)	• Understand and practice different reading strategies • Predict the content of a text by using visuals • Use a synopsis to preview the important information in a text • Identify the main ideas of a text • Understand the details that support the main ideas	• Guess the meaning of words from the context • Understand and use antonyms and word forms • Use dictionary entries to choose the correct meaning of words for the context • Recognize and learn the connotations of words • Use the Vocabulary list at the end of the chapter to review the words, phrases, and idioms learned in the chapter • Use this vocabulary in the After You Read speaking and writing activities
6 PUBLIC ART: Experiencing Familiar Places in a New Way **Theme:** How public art can influence and change our experience **Reading One:** *What Is Public Art?* (an article) **Reading Two:** *Christo and Jeanne-Claude* (a biography)	• Understand and practice different reading strategies • Preview a text using visuals • Scan a text for specific facts • Identify the thesis statement to get the main idea of a text • Identify or complete the main ideas of a text • Understand the details that support the main ideas	• Guess the meaning of words from the context • Understand and use synonyms, antonyms, and word forms • Recognize and use collocations • Sort words by their usage • Use the Vocabulary list at the end of the chapter to review the words, phrases, and idioms learned in the chapter • Use this vocabulary in the After You Read speaking and writing activities

NOTE-TAKING	CRITICAL THINKING	SPEAKING/WRITING
• Use underlining to identify key words and important facts in a reading	• Express opinions and support your opinions with examples from a text or from your own experience and culture • Analyze and evaluate information • Infer information not explicit in a text • Draw conclusions • Interpret quotes and how they relate to a text • Make connections between ideas	• Write a list and discuss your ideas with a partner • Discuss how elephants and humans are similar • Discuss whether you would support the elephant orphanage with donations • Choose one of the topics and write a paragraph or two about it
• Use circling and underlining to distinguish between two sides of an issue or two points of view • Sort the words and phrases for each side of an issue into a chart	• Answer questions based on information in a story or on your own experience and culture • Express your opinions and support them with examples from a story • Infer information not explicit in a story • Draw conclusions • Find correlations between two texts • Make connections between ideas	• Write a letter from the point of view of one of the students in the lesson • Discuss the issue of discrimination and where it comes from • Discuss the merits of participating in the lesson • Choose one of the topics and write a paragraph or two about it
• Use underlining to identify key words and phrases in a reading • Use those key words and phrases to summarize the main point of a reading	• Analyze and evaluate information • Infer information not explicit in a text • Imagine how public art might affect your daily life • Find correlations between two texts • Make connections between ideas • Synthesize information and ideas	• Discuss the merits of public art • Discuss the possible benefits and drawbacks for a community when large-scale artwork is installed • Write an interview with the artist Christo • Choose one of the topics and write a paragraph or two about it

CHAPTER	READING	VOCABULARY
7 SOCIOLOGY: The Bystander Effect **Theme:** What makes people help one another in emergency or dangerous situations **Reading One:** *Why and How Do We Help?* (a magazine article) **Reading Two:** *Case Studies* (two case studies)	• Understand and practice different reading strategies • Skim a text to preview the topic • Scan a text to find specific facts • Identify the main ideas of a text • Understand the details that support the main ideas	• Guess the meaning of words from the context • Understand and use synonyms, antonyms, and parts of speech • Recognize and use collocations • Sort words by parts of speech • Use the Vocabulary list at the end of the chapter to review the words, phrases, and idioms learned in the chapter • Use this vocabulary in the After You Read speaking and writing activities
8 GOVERNMENT: Interpreting the Law **Theme:** How the Supreme Court works to protect the rights of all Americans **Reading One:** *Our Supreme Court—An Introduction* (a book excerpt) **Reading Two:** *Supreme Court Justice Sonia Sotomayor* (a biography)	• Understand and practice different reading strategies • Preview a text using a diagram • Identify the type of text to prepare for the reading • Identify the topic sentence to determine the main idea • Complete the main ideas of a text • Understand the details that support the main ideas	• Guess the meaning of words from the context • Understand and use synonyms and word forms • Recognize and learn the connotations of words • Use dictionary entries to choose the correct meaning of words for the context • Use the Vocabulary list at the end of the chapter to review the words, phrases, and idioms learned in the chapter • Use this vocabulary in the After You Read speaking and writing activities

NOTE-TAKING	CRITICAL THINKING	SPEAKING/WRITING
• Use underlining and margin notes to identify the answers to *wh-* questions	• Express your opinions and support them with examples from a text or from your own experience and culture • Analyze and evaluate information • Infer information not explicit in a text • Draw conclusions • Hypothesize about someone else's thought process • Relate broad themes to specific situations • Find correlations between two texts • Make connections between ideas	• Write an interview with a psychologist studying the bystander effect • Write an interview between a newspaper reporter and Wesley Autry • Discuss whether the bystander effect holds true today, given the advances in technology • Discuss how society can reduce the bystander effect • Choose one of the topics and write a paragraph or two about it
• Create a timeline to remember the sequence of events in a person's life	• Express your opinions and support them with examples from a text or from your own experience and culture • Analyze and evaluate information • Infer information not explicit in a text • Draw conclusions • Find correlations between two texts • Make connections between ideas	• Write questions you would use to interview a potential Supreme Court justice • Discuss the challenges of being a Supreme Court justice • Research and write about a current Supreme Court justice • Discuss in a small group whether judges should have jobs for life • Choose one of the topics and write a paragraph or two about it

CHAPTER	READING	VOCABULARY
9 ECONOMICS: Bartering in the 21st Century **Theme:** How to exchange goods and services without using money **Reading One:** *Swap Tree—Simple, Easy Online Trading* (an online article) **Reading Two:** *Heidemarie Schwermer* (a biography)	• Understand and practice different reading strategies • Predict the content of a text from the title • Predict the content of a text by using visuals such as photos • Identify or complete the main ideas of a text • Understand the details that support the main ideas	• Understand and use synonyms, antonyms, and word forms • Guess the meaning of words from the context • Recognize and learn the connotations of words • Recognize and use prepositions • Use the Vocabulary list at the end of the chapter to review the words, phrases, and idioms learned in the chapter • Use this vocabulary in the After You Read speaking and writing activities
10 NEUROLOGY: The Brain **Theme:** How the brain contributes to laughter **Reading One:** *Why Can't You Tickle Yourself?* (a book excerpt) **Reading Two:** *Laughter and the Brain* (an online article)	• Understand and practice different reading strategies • Scan a text to answer a question in the title • Predict the type of text to prepare for the reading • Identify or complete the main ideas of a text • Understand the details that support the main ideas	• Guess the meaning of words from the context • Understand and use synonyms, antonyms, prefixes, and parts of speech • Recognize and learn the connotations of words • Use dictionary entries to determine the correct meaning of a phrasal verb in context • Use the Vocabulary list at the end of the chapter to review the words, phrases, and idioms learned in the chapter • Use this vocabulary in the After You Read speaking and writing activities

NOTE-TAKING	CRITICAL THINKING	SPEAKING/WRITING
• Use underlining to identify important facts in a text	• Express your opinions and support them with examples from a text or from your own experience and culture • Infer information not explicit in a text • Draw conclusions • Hypothesize about someone else's point of view • Make connections between ideas • Synthesize information and ideas	• Track your spending and write a paragraph answering the questions • In a small group, discuss whether you would have agreed to be part of the experiment to live without money • Discuss what you would miss most about living without money • Choose one of the topics and write a paragraph or two about it
• Use a chart to categorize notes in the two areas discussed in the reading	• Express your opinions and support them with examples from a text or from your own experience and culture • Analyze and evaluate information • Infer information not explicit in a text • Draw conclusions • Find correlations between two texts • Make connections between ideas • Synthesize information and ideas	• Discuss the merits of laughter in treating patients • Write about whether humor and comedy would be used in hospitals in your native country • Write about someone who is funny and what makes them so funny • Discuss the quotes about laughter • Choose one of the topics and write a paragraph or two about it

ACKNOWLEDGMENTS

I'd like to thank Massimo Rubini for inviting me to be a part of this exciting endeavor. His guidance has been extremely valuable. I would also like to thank Robert Cohen, Judy Miller, and Kim Sanabria for providing their creative, clear prototype units, and Lorraine Smith for her enthusiasm and collaboration on this series. Your ideas and dedication have inspired me from the onset of this project. It has been a privilege to work with such seasoned authors, and I will always cherish your willingness to share your ideas with me.

The optimism, patience, and careful attention to detail of my editor Mary Rich are gifts beyond description. Working with Mary has been such a pleasurable and meaningful learning experience. It is with utmost respect and admiration that I thank Mary from the bottom of my heart.

My sincere thanks also go to Amy McCormick, for her support and executive decision-making; to Rosa Chapinal, for her devoted efforts throughout the permissions process; to Jill Krupnik, for her work in negotiating complex permissions contracts; and to Jane Lieberth, for her very thorough and close reading of our manuscript in the production phase.

I would also like to express my thanks to my colleagues at the American Language Program at Columbia University. Working with such creative experts in the field is a gift. I thank my wonderful students from whom I have learned and continue to learn so much.

Finally, it is with heartfelt appreciation that I thank my husband, Lucas, and son, Justin. Your love, patience, and support made it possible for me to write this book.

Reviewers

The publisher would like to thank the following reviewers for their many helpful comments.

Jeff Bette, Naugatuck Valley Community College, Waterbury, Connecticut; **Kevin Knight**, Japan; **Melissa Parisi**, Westchester Community College, Valhalla, New York; **Jason Tannenbaum**, Pace University, Bronx, New York; **Christine Tierney**, Houston Community College, Stafford, Texas; **Kerry Vrabel**, GateWay Community College, Phoenix, Arizona.

CHAPTER 1

HEALTH SCIENCES: The Therapeutic Effects of Animals

HEALTH SCIENCES: the study of medicine, nutrition, and other health-related issues and their possible effects on both humans and animals

OBJECTIVES

To read academic texts, you need to master certain skills.

In this chapter, you will:

- Preview and predict the content of a text using visuals

- Preview and predict the content of a text from its title

- Guess the meaning of words from the context

- Determine whether a word has a positive or negative meaning

- Identify word forms from location in the sentence

- Use a dictionary to find noun forms of verbs

- Use underlining to identify numbers and summarize a text

Consider These Questions

Discuss the questions in a small group.

1. What kind of animal makes the best pet?

2. Why do you think this animal is a good pet?

READING ONE: In the Presence of Animals

A Warm-Up

Check (✓) the statements you think are true about dogs.

☐ **1.** They help people who are sick get better.

☐ **2.** They make people feel relaxed.

☐ **3.** They are good listeners.

☐ **4.** They are good pets for people of all ages.

B Reading Strategy

Predicting Content Using Visuals

Predicting is a very important pre-reading skill. When you **predict**, you make a guess about something based on the information you have. Predicting helps prepare the reader for the reading experience that is to come. Pictures in a text can often help you predict what the text is about.

Look at the picture in the reading. What do you think is going on? Circle one of the choices and discuss your answer with a partner.

    a. a dog gets sick and goes to the hospital

    b. a dog visits a sick person in the hospital

    c. a dog cannot be separated from his owner

Now read the text to find out if your prediction was correct.

In the Presence of Animals

By Sarah Burke in *Science and Society*

1   As far back as the 1790s, the owners of a senior citizens' home in York, England, **encouraged** patients to spend time with farm animals, believing that this would help their mental state[1] more than the sometimes **harsh** therapies[2] used on the mentally ill at the time. In recent years, scientists have finally begun to find **proof** that contact with animals can increase a sick person's chance of **survival** and has been shown to lower heart rate, **calm** upset children, and get people to start a conversation.

2   Scientists think that animal companionship[3] is **beneficial** because animals are accepting and attentive,[4] and they don't **criticize** or give orders. Animals also have a **unique** ability to get people to be more social. Visitors to nursing homes, for example, get more social responses from patients when they come with animal companions, researchers have found.

3   Not only do people seem happier when animals are nearby, but they may also live longer. Studies show that a year after heart **surgery**, survival rates for heart patients were higher for those with pets in their homes than those without pets. **Elderly** people with pets make fewer trips to doctors than those who are without animal companions, possibly because animals lessen **loneliness**. A professor of public health at UCLA says that pet ownership might provide a new form of "low-cost health intervention."[5]

---

[1] *mental state:* emotional condition

[2] *therapies:* treatments

[3] *companionship:* friendship

[4] *accepting and attentive:* agreeable and caring

[5] *intervention:* the act of preventing something undesirable (unwanted)

COMPREHENSION

A Main Ideas

Read each statement. Decide if it is *True* or *False* according to the reading. Check (✓) the appropriate box. If it is false, change it to make it true. Discuss your answers with a partner.

	TRUE	FALSE
1. The first paragraph is ONLY about the effects of animals on people with mental illness in the past.	☐	☐
2. Animals help people communicate more.	☐	☐
3. Because people with animals are not as lonely as people without pets, their health is better.	☐	☐

B Close Reading

Complete each sentence with a phrase from the list on the right.

_____ **1.** Spending time with animals can

_____ **2.** Animals are different from people because

_____ **3.** When visitors bring pets to the hospital,

_____ **4.** After a big operation,

_____ **5.** Older people who have pets go to

_____ **6.** Older people with pets in their lives

a. patients talk more.

b. often live longer.

c. they cannot tell us their opinions.

d. patients with pets get better faster.

e. the doctor less often.

f. make a person's heart rate slower and relax children who are upset.

VOCABULARY

A **Connotations**

Some words have **feelings** connected to them depending on how they are used in a sentence. These feelings, or **connotations**, can be **positive** (good or useful) or **negative** (bad or harmful).

Look at each word. Find the word in the reading. Decide whether it has a *Positive* or *Negative* meaning. Check the appropriate box. Discuss your answers with a partner.

	POSITIVE	NEGATIVE
1. encouraged	☐	☐
2. harsh	☐	☐
3. survival	☐	☐
4. calm	☐	☐
5. beneficial	☐	☐
6. criticize	☐	☐
7. loneliness	☐	☐
8. unique	☐	☐

B **Definitions**

Find each word in the reading and match it with its meaning.

_____ 1. encouraged   a. unpleasant

_____ 2. harsh   b. say what faults someone or something has

_____ 3. proof   c. an operation by a doctor

_____ 4. survival   d. old

_____ 5. calm   e. urged someone to do something

_____ 6. beneficial   f. act of continuing to live

_____ 7. unique   g. unhappy feeling when by oneself

_____ 8. elderly   h. special, rare

_____ 9. loneliness   i. make relaxed

_____ 10. surgery   j. facts

_____ 11. criticize   k. positive

> **Nouns** are words that refer to people, places, things, qualities, actions, and ideas. Nouns can come **after** articles (*a/an, the*) or possessive pronouns (*my, your, his/her/its, our, their*), prepositions, and adjectives or **before** or after verbs. Many nouns end in *-ness*, *-ity*, or *-tion*.
>
> **Adjectives** are words that describe nouns or pronouns. They are placed **before** nouns or after the verbs *be, seem, feel,* and *look*. Many adjectives end in *-able* and *-ial*.
>
> **Verbs** are words that describe actions, experiences, or states. They follow nouns and often come **after** *to* as in "to go" (the infinitive).

Look at the words in bold and decide if they are nouns, adjectives, or verbs. Write the part of speech on the line next to the sentence. Use the explanations in the box above to help you make your decision.

_____*verb*_____ 1. The owners of a senior citizens' home **encouraged** patients to spend time with farm animals.

_____ 2. In the past, there were many **harsh** therapies for people with mental illness.

_____ 3. His chance of **survival** was better because he had a pet.

_____ 4. Sometimes, pets **calm** upset children.

_____ 5. Animal companionship is **beneficial**.

_____ 6. **Elderly** people sometimes feel lonely.

_____ 7. People with pets often have less **loneliness**.

_____ 8. **Surgery** is a serious medical treatment.

CRITICAL THINKING

Discuss the questions with a partner. Be prepared to share your answers with the class.

1. The author puts the date **1790** in the first paragraph. This is a **fact** about how long ago people began to think animals were good for therapy. What other words in paragraph 1 give the reader the idea that this article is about facts and not opinions?

2. What other words in paragraphs 2 and 3 tell us that this reading is about facts more than opinions?

3. Why do you think the article presents facts and not opinions?

A Warm-Up

Read the quotation. Check (✓) the sentences that have the same meaning as the quote.

"An animal's eyes have the power to speak a great language."

—*Martin Buber,* philosopher

☐ **1.** Animals communicate a lot of feelings with their eyes.

☐ **2.** Animals use their eyes to speak to us.

☐ **3.** When animals look at us, we feel connected to them.

B Reading Strategy

Predicting Content from the Title

Predicting is a very important pre-reading skill. When you **predict**, you make a guess about something based on the information you have. Predicting helps prepare the reader for the reading experience that is to come. The title of a text can often help you predict what the text is about.

The title of the reading is "Canine Companions May Help Kids Learn to Read." With a partner, write two predictions about the content of the reading.

1. _____

2. _____

Now read the article to find out if your predictions were correct.

Canine Companions May Help Kids Learn to Read

By Maryann Mott for *National Geographic News*

1   Walk into a Salt Lake City public library on a Saturday afternoon and you
    might see something you didn't **expect**: children reading books to dogs.
    Three years ago, Intermountain Therapy Animals (ITA) started the R.E.A.D.®
    (Reading Education Assistance Dogs) program at the suggestion of
    board member Sandi Martin, a nurse and a long-time supporter of pets in
    hospitals, who had seen the positive effect animals can have on mentally
    and physically challenged[1] children. If therapy dogs help those children,
    thought Martin, who loves to read, then perhaps they can help kids who are
    struggling with reading, too.

2   The program is simple. For about 30 minutes each week, kids from five to
    nine years old read aloud to dogs of all shapes and sizes. The people **in
    charge of** the dogs sit nearby to help. Martin says children are more willing
    to read to dogs than to their classmates, in part because kids who stumble
    over[2] new words know their furry friends won't make fun of them. As a result,
    children's reading skills improve and their **self-esteem** grows.

---

[1] *mentally or physically challenged:* having a more difficult time with mental or physical
   skills than the average person

[2] *stumble over:* to have difficulty doing something; hesitate

3 Initially the R.E.A.D.® program was held in the main branch[3] of the Salt Lake City library, but it has become so popular that all six branches now hold weekly sessions. Last year more than 500 children **participated**. Learning while having fun is what makes the program successful. ITA Executive Director Kathy Klotz explains that when people of all ages participate in therapy with animals, they stop thinking about what they can't do and **focus on** being with the dog.

4 ITA, based in Salt Lake City, has 250 Pet Partner® teams, 45 of which participate in the R.E.A.D.® program. To enter the program, teams go through a two-hour training course. Dogs are taught to look at the children's faces or at the books they are reading.

5 Handlers, the people who take care of the dogs, are given instructions. For example, instead of asking a child what a word means, the handler may say: "Rover[4] doesn't know what that word means. Can you tell him?" This **takes the pressure off** the child if he or she doesn't know the answer, says Klotz.

6 Dogs also have a natural calming effect on humans. Studies have shown blood pressure[5] and anxiety levels[6] drop when people **are around** pets. "If kids who don't read well can relax enough to focus on learning, hopefully their reading will improve and they'll want to continue to read just for the pleasure of it," explains Martin.

---

[3] *branch:* something that is part of a larger system

[4] *Rover:* the name of a dog

[5] *blood pressure:* the measure of the force of the blood against artery walls. High blood pressure is a sign of a health problem.

[6] *anxiety levels:* how much stress a person experiences

(A) Close Reading

Circle the word(s) that completes the sentence correctly.

1. Children read **silently/out loud** to dogs.

2. Children like reading to the dogs because they **will/won't** laugh at them.

3. The R.E.A.D.® program is growing **quickly/slowly**.

4. Kids in the R.E.A.D.® program focus on **themselves/the dog**.

5. In the training program, dogs are taught to look at the **kids'/handler's** faces or at the books they are reading.

6. Handlers **ask/don't ask** kids what words mean.

7. If kids can relax more, their reading **will/won't improve,** and they will want to keep reading.

(B) Main Ideas

Circle ALL the correct answers for each question.

1. Who is this reading about?
   a. nurses
   b. dogs
   c. people who are responsible for the dogs
   d. children

2. What is the R.E.A.D.® program about?
   a. teaching dogs to read
   b. training dogs
   c. helping children become better readers
   d. increasing children's confidence

3. Where is this program?
   a. at schools
   b. in hospitals
   c. at libraries
   d. in parks

4. How often does this program occur?
   a. once a week
   b. twice a week
   c. for 30 minutes
   d. for 1 hour

5. Why is this program successful?

    a. It's fun.

    b. It's simple.

    c. It's relaxing.

    d. It's satisfying.

VOCABULARY

 Guessing from Context

> Looking up every unfamiliar word in the dictionary is not an effective way to read. It is much better to **guess the meaning of unfamiliar words from the rest of the sentence or paragraph (the context)** and keep reading. Some words in particular can help you guess. No one guesses correctly all the time, but practice makes all the difference. You can use the dictionary after you get the main idea of the reading.

Read each sentence and guess the meaning of the word in bold from the context. Then match the word with its meaning from the box below. Circle the words in the sentence that helped you guess the word's meaning.

_f_   1. I was really surprised to see dogs in libraries. I didn't **expect** this.

_____   2. The five-year-old boy was **struggling** with his homework because he'd been sick and missed a week of school.

_____   3. The handlers **are in charge of** the dogs. That is, they are responsible for the dogs' behavior.

_____   4. The eight-year-old girl was reading much better after a few months in the program, and she became much more confident. As a result, her **self-esteem** grew.

_____   5. Hundreds of children **participated** in the R.E.A.D.® program last year. They had more fun reading because they had joined that program.

_____   6. The children are able to **focus on** the dog, so they are not giving their attention to their problems.

_____   7. If we **take the pressure off** of children, they can relax and perform better.

_____   8. I like to **be around** my dog. When I am with her, life is calm.

a. self-respect	**d.** are in control	**g.** be with
b. having a hard time	**e.** lower the stress	**h.** concentrate on
c. took part	**f.** think I would see	

B Vocabulary in Context

Complete the conversation between Ms. Kruchin, the teacher, and Mrs. Sugimoto, the parent, with words or phrases from the box. There is one extra word or phrase.

are in charge of	expected	participating	struggle
be around	focuses	self-esteem	takes the pressure off

MS. KRUCHIN: So, Mrs. Sugimoto. How do you like the R.E.A.D.® program? Is it different from what you

_____expected_____?
1.

MRS. SUGIMOTO: Yes! It's a lot of fun. I never thought it was possible for reading to be relaxing for my daughter, but the dogs are so cute and really good listeners. When she

_____ on the dogs, she
2.
doesn't _____ as much.
3.

MS. KRUCHIN: I'm so happy she likes to

_____ dogs. It sounds like
4.
she feels comfortable with them, and this helps her not to get nervous when she reads, right?

MRS. SUGIMOTO: Right. Reading to dogs

_____ her. She knows
5.
they won't make fun of her if she makes a mistake, so she feels more confident when she reads.

MS. KRUCHIN: That's amazing! I can see how her

_____ is growing.
6.

MRS. SUGIMOTO: Thanks. I'm really glad she is

_____ in this program.
7.

Fill in the chart with the correct noun for each verb. Use a dictionary if necessary.

	NOUN	VERB
1.		expect
2.		struggle
3.		participate

NOTE-TAKING: Underlining Numbers

1 Go back to the reading. Underline the numbers and the nouns that follow them.

EXAMPLE:

> 1 Walk into a Salt Lake City public library on a Saturday afternoon and you might see something you **didn't expect**: children reading books to dogs. Three years ago, Intermountain Therapy Animals (ITA) started the R.E.A.D.® (Reading Education Assistance Dogs) program at the suggestion of board member Sandi Martin, a nurse and a long-time supporter of pets in hospitals, who had seen the positive effect animals can have on mentally and physically challenged children.

2 Complete the summary with the numbers you underlined while taking notes on the reading.

Intermountain Therapy Animals' (ITA) R.E.A.D.® program has been

around for _____*three*_____ years. Each week children from
                        1.

_____ to _____ years old read
         2.   3.

to dogs to gain more confidence so that they can improve their reading

skills. Each kid reads to a dog for _____ minutes.
                                              4.

The program has become so popular that it expanded from one library

to _____ branches in Salt Lake City. In 2002 there
         5.

were _____ children participating in the program.
         6.

ITA works with _____ Pet Partner® teams, and
                        7.

_____ of these teams take part in the R.E.A.D.® program.
         8.

CRITICAL THINKING

Discuss the questions in a small group. Be prepared to share your ideas with the class.

1. The R.E.A.D.® program is very successful with children from five to nine years old. Would this program be effective with older children from 10 to 13, for example? Explain why.

2. The author of Reading One writes: "Animals are accepting and attentive, and they don't criticize or give orders." Find a sentence in paragraph 2 of Reading Two to support why the writer of this article would or would not agree with this idea.

3. Why are dogs taught to look at the children's faces or the books they are reading?

4. Why do the handlers pretend the dog is asking the question?

AFTER YOU READ

WRITING ACTIVITY

Choose one of the topics and write a paragraph about it. Use at least five of the words and phrases you studied in the chapter (for a complete list, go to page 15).

1. Imagine you walked into the library and saw children reading to dogs. Describe what you see and how you feel. Give as many details as possible.

2. Do you think everyone should have a pet? Explain your opinion.

DISCUSSION AND WRITING TOPICS

Discuss these topics in a small group. Choose one of them and write a paragraph or two about it. Use the vocabulary from the chapter.

1. Is it common for people in your home country to have pets? If so, what are the most popular pets, and why are they popular?

2. What other animals might be used for therapeutic purposes? Give specific details and examples to support your choice.

VOCABULARY

Nouns	Verbs	Adjectives	Phrases and Idioms
loneliness	calm	beneficial*	be around
proof	criticize	elderly	be in charge of
self-esteem	encourage	harsh	focus on
surgery	expect	unique*	take the pressure
survival*	participate*		off
	struggle		

* = AWL (Academic Word List) item

SELF-ASSESSMENT

In this chapter you learned to:

○ Preview and predict the content of a text using visuals

○ Preview and predict the content of a text from its title

○ Guess the meaning of words from the context

○ Determine whether a word has a positive or negative meaning

○ Identify word forms from location in the sentence

○ Use a dictionary to find noun forms of verbs

○ Use underlining to identify numbers and summarize a text

What can you do well? ✓

What do you need to practice more? ✓

CHAPTER 2

PSYCHOLOGY:
Dealing with Change

PSYCHOLOGY: the study of the mind and how it works

OBJECTIVES

To read academic texts, you need to master certain skills.

In this chapter, you will:

- Skim a text to identify main ideas and type of text

- Guess the meaning of words from the context

- Use new vocabulary

- Understand parts of speech

- Understand and use synonyms

- Understand collocations, or how words go together in English

- Use an organizer to take notes

Consider These Questions

Discuss the picture in a small group.

1. How would you describe the glass? Is it half full or half empty?

2. An **optimist** is person who believes good things will happen in the future, while a **pessimist** believes bad things will happen in the future. Based on this definition, would an optimist see the glass as half empty or half full?

READING ONE: Young Football Players Injured, but Not Forgotten

(A) Warm-Up

Discuss the meaning of the quote with a partner.

"When one door of happiness closes, another opens; but often we look so long at the closed door that we do not see the one which has been opened for us."

— *Helen Keller, American author and educator who was blind and deaf, 1880–1968*

(B) Reading Strategy

Skimming

Reading something quickly to find the main idea or important facts is called **skimming**. To **skim,** read as fast as you can without stopping.

Skim the reading for the main ideas. Then check (✓) the true statements.

This story is about . . .

☐ **1.** someone who likes football but cannot play anymore

☐ **2.** how a father helps his son

☐ **3.** a group that helps young, injured football players

Now read the text to find out more.

Young Football Players Injured, but Not Forgotten

By Kathleen Toner, *CNN*

February 3, 2011

1 Two moments have changed Eddie Canales' life. Both happened on the football field. The first happened almost 10 years ago. It was November 2, 2001, and Canales was watching his son's football game in San Marcos, Texas. Chris Canales, a high school senior, had three offers to play college football, and that night, he was having the game of his life, but with four minutes left in the game something **went wrong**. "I could hear my teammates saying, 'Chris, come on, let's go,' " Chris, now 26, remembered. "And I couldn't move."

2 At the hospital, doctors told Eddie and his wife that their son had suffered a spinal cord injury.[1] If Chris lived, he'd probably never be able to move anything below his shoulders. Chris almost died twice during those early days. But he started to get better. Eddie quit his job to become his full-time caregiver. The family **adjusted** to their new **circumstances**, but Eddie, 55, said it wasn't easy. "You don't want to even think that your son may never walk again," he said. "That was a hard pill to swallow."

3 Near the first anniversary of his injury, Chris was **depressed**. To **cheer him up**, Eddie invited him out to do something he'd always enjoyed — watching high school football. It was the first time Chris had been out to watch a game since his injury. But that afternoon, as they watched, a player went down[2] and couldn't move. Eddie and Chris knew immediately that it was a spinal cord injury. "Chris turned to me and said, 'Dad, we've got to go help him,' " Eddie recalled.

4 In that moment, Eddie's life changed again: He found his **mission.** He and Chris visited the injured player and his family in the hospital, and within months, Gridiron Heroes — a nonprofit[3] that helps athletes who've suffered spinal cord injuries while playing high school football — was born. It now includes 19 injured players in Texas. Many spinal injury organizations raise money for medical research. But from the start, Eddie wanted to give **emotional** support to injured athletes and their families. Whenever a new player joins the group, he and Chris drive to visit them no matter where they live in the state. Eddie helps the families face many emotional, financial, and practical issues, while Chris encourages and **mentors** the athletes. "We try to provide information, **inspiration,** and hope," Eddie said. "We want to make sure they don't feel alone."

---

[1] *spinal cord injury:* damage to the long string of nerves that go from the brain down the back, through the spine

[2] *went down:* fell on the ground

[3] *a nonprofit:* an organization that uses the money it earns to help people instead of making a profit

COMPREHENSION

A **Main Ideas**

Circle the word(s) that correctly completes the sentence.

1. Chris had a serious accident in **high school/college**.

2. The doctors told Chris's parents he might never be able to move his **head/body** again.

3. Chris' dad quit his job because he **couldn't work/wanted to take care of his son**.

4. Chris' dad took him to see a football game **five years/one year** after his injury.

5. When Chris saw the football player fall, he **wanted/didn't want** to help him.

6. Chris and his father started an organization to give injured athletes **physical/emotional** support.

B **Close Reading**

Read each statement. Decide if it is *True* or *False* according to the reading. Check (✓) the appropriate box. If it is false, change it to make it true. Discuss your answers with a partner.

	TRUE	FALSE
1. In paragraph 1, the author writes: "Chris Canales, a high school senior, had **three offers to play college football**, and that night, he was **having the game of his life**." This means that Chris was such a great football player in high school that three colleges wanted to give him a scholarship, and he was playing really well during that game.	☐	☐
2. In the last sentence in paragraph 2, Eddie, Chris' father said: "**That** was a hard pill to swallow." *A hard pill to swallow* describes a situation that is very difficult to accept. In this sentence *that* refers to Eddie quitting his job.	☐	☐
3. When Chris realized he could help another football player who got injured, he opened a new door to happiness.	☐	☐
4. Chris speaks on the phone to injured football players who live far away from him to give them advice.	☐	☐

VOCABULARY

A **Guessing from Context**

Find each word or phrase in the reading and match it with its meaning.

_i_ 1. went wrong   a. advises

___ 2. adjusted   b. slowly became comfortable with

___ 3. circumstances   c. very sad

___ 4. depressed   d. motivation

___ 5. cheer up   e. try to help someone feel happy

___ 6. mission   f. conditions

___ 7. emotional   g. related to feelings

___ 8. mentors   h. goal

___ 9. inspiration   i. did not happen the way it was supposed to

B **Collocations**

> When **words** are **used together regularly**, they become a pair and are called **collocations**. The word pairing is not for grammatical reasons, but because of the association with each other. For example, we say "fast food" but "a quick meal."

Complete each sentence with the word that makes a collocation with the word in bold. Go back to the reading to check if necessary.

emotional	found	new	provide

1. Her _____ **circumstances** made it difficult for her to find a job.

2. When he _____ his new **mission**, Chris felt hopeful.

3. _____ **support** is very important during times of change.

4. Helen Keller's quote might _____ **inspiration** for many people.

CRITICAL THINKING

Discuss the questions in a small group. Be prepared to share your answers with the class.

1. Do you think Chris and his family would agree with Helen Keller's quote at the beginning of this chapter? Why?

2. If you could meet Chris and his parents, what question would you ask each of them?

3. With a partner, take turns asking and answering the questions you wrote. When you answer, imagine that you are Chris, Eddie, or Chris's mom and use the information from the reading as well as your imagination to respond.

READING TWO: Who Moved My Cheese?

A Warm-Up

Think about a time in your life when you were faced with a big change. Spend a few minutes answering these questions. Then tell a partner about that time of your life.

1. What was the change?

2. When did it happen? How old were you?

3. Where were you?

4. Were you alone or with family or friends?

5. Did this change happen slowly or fast?

B Reading Strategy

Identifying Type of Text

Identifying the **type of text** you are about to read will help you determine what kind of information you can expect to find in that text.

Skim the reading. Circle the correct answer(s) to each question. Sometimes more than one answer is possible.

1. Skim paragraph 1. What type of text is this?
   a. an opinion article
   b. a letter
   c. a book review

2. Where might you find this type of information?
   a. in the newspaper
   b. on the radio
   c. on websites where books are sold

3. What type of information is usually found in a book review?
   a. whether the reviewer liked it
   b. the price
   c. the ending of the story

4. Why do people read book reviews?
   a. to find out why people like the book
   b. to get a general idea about what the book is about
   c. to get the reviewer's opinion about the book

Now read the review to find out more about *Who Moved My Cheese*?

Who Moved My Cheese?

October 1, 2010

1   *Who Moved My Cheese?* is a book about four characters. Sniff[1] and Scurry[2] are mice, and Hem and Haw[3] are people. They move around the maze to find cheese to eat. They find a cheese station so full of cheese that they think it is enough to last a lifetime. Suddenly, all the cheese disappears from that station, leaving the four **stunned**. The reality is, it had been gradually **decreasing**, but they had failed to notice it. How they react to this situation is the remaining part of the story.

2   Cheese here is a symbol for things we **pursue** in life, such as a job or a relationship. The cheese having disappeared in this parable[4] represents change.

3   Sniff and Scurry are mice, and so have smaller brains than humans. We tend to think mice are less intelligent than human beings. But in reality, smaller brain implies lesser complexity. They don't plan. They act. Sniff and Scurry are ready to handle the cheese crisis. Without second thoughts, they get back to looking for more.

4   Hem and Haw are a little bit too **complicated**. They can't help using their brains more. Hem, in particular and as the name suggests, is someone who is afraid of change. Is this not the situation in which we find ourselves most of the time?

5   The two little people, however, mope around,[5] blaming someone for moving their cheese. They claim they don't deserve to be in such a situation. They are not prepared to look again for more, even though it is their only source of survival. Finally, Haw stopped being afraid and went to find new cheese. He left the following messages for Hem:

6   They keep moving the cheese. (Change happens)

7   Get ready for the cheese to move. (**Anticipate** change)

8   Smell the cheese often so you know when it's getting old. (**Monitor** change)

9   The more quickly you **let go of** old cheese, the sooner you can enjoy new cheese. (**Adapt** to change quickly)

10   Move with the cheese. (Change) **Savor** the adventure and enjoy the taste of new cheese. (Enjoy change)

(continued on next page)

---

[1] *sniff:* to breathe in through your nose in order to smell something

[2] *scurry:* to move very quickly with small steps

[3] *hem and haw:* to hesitate and to avoid saying something directly

[4] *parable:* a short, simple story that teaches a moral or religious lesson

[5] *mope around:* to pity oneself and feel sad, without trying to be happier

11   Someone will keep moving the cheese. (Be ready to enjoy change quickly, and enjoy it every time)

12   Ask yourself: "What would I do if I were not afraid?" Now get going, because a "good enough" solution to a problem is fine. It is much better, in fact, than a "no-solution." Even the best would be futile[6] if it comes too late. In short, this book, *Who Moved My Cheese*? is very much worth[7] the read.

_____

[6] ***futile:*** having no chance of being effective or successful

[7] ***worth:*** valuable, interesting, helpful

COMPREHENSION

Ⓐ Main Ideas

Circle the letter of the correct answer.

1. This story is about _____.

    a. four mice

    b. four people

    c. two mice and two people

    d. cheese

2. The story takes place _____.

    a. in a station

    b. in a maze

    c. at work

    d. in a store

3. When Hem and Haw discover that their cheese is gone, they blame someone for taking their cheese and _____.

   a. start looking for new cheese

   b. get into an argument

   c. feel sorry for themselves

   d. ask the mice for help

4. Haw finally decides to _____.

   a. stay with Hem

   b. look for the mice

   c. find new cheese

   d. make a plan

5. Haw is able to make his decision because _____.

   a. he's really hungry

   b. he's tired of listening to Hem complain

   c. he wants to find the mice

   d. he stops being afraid

B **Close Reading**

Read each statement. Decide if it is *True* or *False* according to the reading. Check (✓) the appropriate box. If it is false, change it to make it true. Discuss your answers with a partner.

	TRUE	FALSE
1. The mice are stunned when the cheese is gone because they didn't realize the amount of cheese was slowly becoming less and less.	☑	☐
2. The cheese represents what is important to us in life, such as relationships and careers.	☐	☐
3. The cheese disappearing represents our laziness.	☐	☐
4. The mice react to the "cheese crisis" (no more cheese) by worrying and not doing anything.	☐	☐
5. The brains of mice and people are very similar.	☐	☐
6. Haw learned that change is a natural part of life and we need to accept it.	☐	☐

(A) Parts of Speech

> **Adjectives** are words that describe nouns or pronouns. They are placed **before** nouns or after the verbs *be, seem, feel,* and *look*. Many adjectives end in *-able* and *-ial*.
>
> **Verbs** are words that describe actions, experiences, or states. They follow nouns and often come **after** *to* as in "to go" (the infinitive).

1 Read the descriptions of adjectives and verbs. Then sort the words in the box according to their parts of speech.

adapt	complicated	let go of	pursue
anticipate	decreasing	monitor	stunned

ADJECTIVES	VERBS
	let go of

2 List the adjectives from 1. Go back to the reading and find the nouns the adjectives describe.

ADJECTIVES	NOUNS
_____	_____
_____	_____
_____	_____

A **synonym** is a word that has the same or a very similar meaning to another word.

Read the sentences. Match the words in bold with a synonym from the list below. Do not use a dictionary. Use the information in the sentences to figure out the meanings of the words. Write the letter of the synonym next to the sentence. There is one extra word.

a. adjust	**f.** expected
b. astonished	**g.** follow
c. check	**h.** ineffective
d. complex	**i.** release
e. declining	

_b_ **1.** I was **stunned** when my parents told me we were moving to a new city. I thought I could finish high school before we moved.

____ **2.** She went to take money out of her bank account, but there was no money left. If she had checked her bank statements, she would have seen her funds had been **decreasing**.

____ **3.** Ahmed moved to the United States to **pursue** his dream. He wanted to get a master's degree from an American university.

____ **4.** Humans are **complicated** creatures and tend to spend a lot of time thinking and planning.

____ **5.** If rain is **anticipated**, it's a good idea to carry an umbrella.

____ **6.** Teachers **monitor** students' progress by giving homework and tests.

____ **7.** Change can be difficult in the beginning, but by being patient, we can gradually **adapt** to it.

____ **8.** If we don't **let go of** the past, we cannot make progress in the present.

C Word Usage

Complete the diary entry with the words from the box.

anticipate	decreasing	monitored	stunned
complicated	let go of	pursue	

Dear Diary,

Today I realized that change isn't bad. It just is. In other words,

life happens, and we find ourselves in different circumstances.

What we do at that moment is important. Today, I was

_____stunned_____ when I suddenly realized I ran out of
1.

cheese. Hem and I started to complain and feel sorry for ourselves. If

we had _____ our food supply, we would have
2.

realized that the amount of cheese was _____.
3.

We didn't _____ the change. Our friends, the
4.

mice, however, just got up and started looking for new cheese. Not

us! We couldn't _____ the problem. Our brains
5.

make us too _____! Finally, a light bulb went
6.

off in my head, and I realized sitting around and blaming others was

useless. So, I got up to _____ my goal and find
7.

new cheese.

Good night,

Haw

NOTE-TAKING: Using an Organizer

> When reading a summary of a book, movie, or play, you can often find the main ideas by asking **wh- questions** such as *when, where, who, what,* and *why.*

Complete the organizer with the main ideas from the reading.

TITLE: Who Moved My Cheese?				
WHEN?	WHERE?	WHO?	WHAT?	WHY?

CRITICAL THINKING

> *Who Moved My Cheese?* is a **parable**. A parable is a short, simple story that teaches a lesson. Parables often contain symbolism to illustrate key ideas. For example, "cheese" in this story symbolizes (represents) things we pursue in life, such as jobs and relationships.

Discuss the questions about some of the other symbolism in the story in a small group. Be prepared to share your ideas with the class.

1. What do you think the names of the four characters in the story symbolize?

2. What does the maze symbolize?

3. What do the following sentences from paragraph 12 mean?

   A "good enough" solution to a problem is fine. It is much better, in fact, than a "no-solution." Even the best would be **futile** if it comes too late.

4. What is the moral of the parable? That is, what does this story teach us?

WRITING ACTIVITY

Write two paragraphs about a change you experienced. Use at least five of the vocabulary words you studied in the chapter (for a complete list, go to page 31).

- **First paragraph:** Describe the change. When summarizing the change, use the *wh-* questions to recall important parts of this event.

- **Second paragraph:** Write about what you learned from the experience and whether you would handle the situation in the same way or differently in the future.

DISCUSSION AND WRITING TOPICS

Discuss these topics in a small group. Choose one of them and write a paragraph about it. Use the vocabulary from the chapter.

1. In your culture, is change seen as something positive or negative? Why?

2. Are you afraid of change? Why or why not?

3. What have you learned about change from these two readings?

It can be stressful to make choices that force change in your life, but it can also be exciting.

VOCABULARY

Nouns	Verbs	Adjectives	Phrases and Idioms
circumstance	adapt*	complicated	cheer up
inspiration	adjust*	depressed*	go wrong
mentor	anticipate*	emotional	let go of
mission	decrease	stunned	
	monitor*		
	pursue*		
	savor		

* = AWL (Academic Word List) item

SELF-ASSESSMENT

In this chapter you learned to:

○ Skim a text to identify main ideas and type of text

○ Guess the meaning of words from the context

○ Use new vocabulary

○ Understand parts of speech

○ Understand and use synonyms

○ Understand collocations, or how words go together in English

○ Use an organizer to take notes

What can you do well? ☑

What do you need to practice more? ☑

CHAPTER 3

LINGUISTICS:
Little-Known Languages

LINGUISTICS: the scientific study of the nature, structure, grammar, and history of the world's languages. A **linguist** is someone who studies languages and linguistics. In ordinary speech, a linguist can also be someone who speaks many languages or who has a large vocabulary.

OBJECTIVES

To write academic texts, you need to master certain skills.

In this chapter, you will:

- Scan a text for numbers

- Read a chart for information

- Identify the parts of an introduction

- Understand and use synonyms

- Understand prefixes and suffixes

- Use a dictionary to find the meaning of vocabulary in context

- Take margin notes to remember the main ideas

Linguists classify languages into different **language families**. The one with the largest number of native speakers is the Indo-European family, which includes languages from India to Europe and North and South America. English is an Indo-European language. English has its roots in Germanic languages but includes many words from Latin and French.

Consider This Chart

Look at the chart. Discuss the questions in a small group.

1. Do you think any one language is more important than another?
2. What makes a language important?
3. What are the advantages of speaking a language many other people speak?

Rank	Language	Speakers (millions)	Where Spoken (major locations)
	MOST WIDELY SPOKEN LANGUAGES IN THE WORLD		
1	Mandarin	1151	China, Malaysia, Taiwan
2	English	1000	USA, UK, Australia, Canada, New Zealand
3	Spanish	500	Mexico, Central and South America, Spain
4	Hindi	490	North and Central India
5	Russian	277	Russia, Central Asia
6	Arabic	255	Middle East, Arabia, North Africa
7	Portuguese	240	Brazil, Portugal, Southern Africa
8	Bengali	215	Bangladesh, Eastern India
9	French	200	France, Canada, West Africa, Central Africa
10	Malay, Indonesian	175	Indonesia, Malaysia, Singapore
11	German	166	Germany, Austria, Central Europe
12	Japanese	132	Japan
13	Farsi (Persian)	110	Iran, Afghanistan, Central Asia
14	Urdu	104	Pakistan, India

© 1997, 2010 KryssTal Link: http://www.krysstal.com/spoken.html

Ⓐ Warm-Up

**A code is a secret way to communicate. This is a coded message in "pig Latin."
Can you guess what it says?**

Endsay oneymay astfay.

1. Can you read this message?

   How to write in this code: Move the first letter of the word to the end of
   the word and add "ay" to it. Example: CODE = ODE + C + AY = ODECAY

2. Now can you read the message? Can you write a message in this code?

3. This code is named "pig Latin," but it's not based on Latin (the language of
   ancient Rome.) It's really based on English. Thomas Jefferson, the writer of
   the Declaration of Independence, wrote part of his diaries in pig Latin. Can
   you write pig Latin messages in other languages that you know? Does the
   code work?

The great painter Leonardo da Vinci used a different code in his writings:

Hold the message up to a mirror. Do you see how the message is readable
when viewed in a mirror?

4. In what situations do you think people would need to use a code?

Scanning

Scanning is useful when looking for specific facts. To **scan**, quickly look over the text to find the necessary information.

The title of the reading is "An Unbreakable Code." The title refers to a secret code used during World War II.

Scan the reading to find the numbers to complete these sentences.

1. In Navajo, one vowel can have _____ pronunciations.

2. There were _____ Navajo Code Talkers with the U.S. Marines in World War II.

3. In _____ the Navajo Code was no longer a secret.

Now read the text to find out more about this secret code.

An Unbreakable Code

1   In most Hollywood movies, the Native American Navajos still fight on horses in the American Southwest. But during World War II, a group of Navajos made their language into a weapon to protect the United States. They were the Navajo Code Talkers, and theirs is one of the few unbroken codes in military history.

2   Navajo was the perfect choice for a secret language. It is very **complex**. One vowel can have up to ten different pronunciations, changing the meaning of any word. In the 1940s, Navajo was an unwritten language. No one outside of the reservation could speak it or understand it.

3   The Navajo Code team had to invent new words to **describe** military equipment. For example, they named ships after fish: *lotso-whale* (battleship), *calo-shark* (destroyer), and *beshloiron-fish* (submarine). When a Code Talker

These are some of the Navajo Code Talkers in the U.S. Marines in 1943. Their code was very valuable in the war effort.

received a message **via** radio, he heard a series of unrelated Navajo words. He would then translate the words into

(continued on next page)

English and use the first letter of each English word to spell the message. The Navajo words *tsah* (<u>n</u>eedle), *wol-la-chee* (<u>a</u>nt), *ah-kh-di-glini* (<u>v</u>ictor), and *tsah-ah-dzoh* (<u>y</u>ucca)[1] spelled *NAVY*.

4 The Code Talkers kept the code a secret. They **memorized** everything. There were no code books. As a result, no ordinary Navajo soldier, if **captured** by the enemy, could understand the code. More than 3,600 Navajos served in World War II, but only 420 were Code Talkers with the U.S. Marines. They coded and decoded battlefield messages

_____

[1] *yucca:* a desert plant with long, pointed leaves on a thick, straight stem

better and faster than any machine. They could encode, transmit, and decode a three-line English message in 20 seconds. Machines of the time required 30 minutes to perform the same job.

5 Even after the war the code **remained** top secret. When they were asked about their role, Code Talkers just said: "I was a radioman." War movies and histories came out without **mentioning** them. The code was never used again and was finally declassified[2] in 1968. Only then did the secret come out.

_____

[2] *declassified:* made public after having been kept secret

COMPREHENSION

 Main Ideas

Read each statement. Decide if it is *True* or *False* according to the reading. Check (✓) the appropriate box. If it is false, change it to make it true. Discuss your answers with a partner.

	TRUE	FALSE
1. Native Americans did a great service for their country.	☐	☐
2. Machine translators worked faster than the Navajos.	☐	☐
3. The Code Talkers had to translate from one language to another.	☐	☐
4. All the Navajos in the U.S. Marines used the code.	☐	☐
5. The code can be used again in the future.	☐	☐

Read the quotes from the reading. Circle the letter of the statement that best explains each quote. Discuss your answers with a partner.

1. "But during World War II, a group of Navajos made their language into a weapon." This sentence means:

   a. The Navajo language included a lot of words about fighting.

   b. The Navajo language had protected the Navajos from the cowboys.

   c. The Navajo language was used in the war effort.

2. "One vowel can have up to 10 different pronunciations." This sentence means:

   a. One vowel can be pronounced in more than 10 different ways.

   b. One vowel can be pronounced in 10 different ways or less.

   c. One vowel can be pronounced in less than 10 different ways.

3. "*Theirs* is one of the few unbroken codes in military history." *Theirs* refers to:

   a. the Navajo Code Talkers

   b. the U.S. Marines

   c. the Navajo language

4. "Only then did the secret come out." This sentence means:

   a. It was at that time that the secret was revealed.

   b. Only the secret code came out.

   c. It was at that time that the secret code was used.

VOCABULARY

A **Synonyms**

Complete each sentence with a word from the box. Use the synonym (a word that means the same) in parentheses to help you select the correct word. Compare answers with a partner

captured	complex	describe	memorized	remain	via

1. Traditional Navajo people _____ *memorized* _____ their history to share
   (remembered)

   with the next generation.

2. In 1864 Kit Carson and the U.S. Army _____
   (caught)

   thousands of Navajo people and made them march 300 miles to New

   Mexico as prisoners on the Long Walk.

3. Books _____ how the U.S. Army burned Navajo
   (tell)

   crops, killed their animals, and destroyed their homes.

4. When the Navajo returned to Arizona, they had to _____
   (stay)

   on a reservation under U.S. government control.

5. The Code Talkers served their country _____ the
   (by way of)

   code, but they couldn't vote in Arizona until 1948.

6. The decision to help their country was _____ for the
   (difficult)

   Navajo because they were not always accepted as full Americans.

B Prefixes

A **prefix** is a group of letters added to the beginning of a word that changes the word's meaning. Knowing what prefixes mean can help you figure out the meanings of words as you read.

The Prefix *Un-*

un- = **not**

In adjectives and adverbs, *un-* is used to show an opposite or negative state:

The Navajo Code remained **unbroken** for many years.
              [not broken]

The Prefix *De-*

de- = **remove from**

In some verbs or adjectives, **de-** means "to remove from something or to remove something from something":

They had to **decode** the message in order to understand it.
    [remove the code from]

Work with a partner to complete this summary of the reading. Circle the correct word.

The Navajo contribution to the United States war effort went almost **mentioned/unmentioned** in American history. The Navajo Code remained **known/unknown** to the other 3,200 Navajo soldiers who were not Code Talkers. The code, like the Navajo language, was **written/unwritten**, and it was memorized only by the Code Talkers. Other Navajos could not decode it, because it contained a series of **related/unrelated** Navajo words. This code remained **breakable/unbreakable** for more than 20 years after the war, until 1968, when the U.S. government **classified/declassified** it and made its secret known to the public.

NOTE-TAKING: Writing Margin Notes

> Writing notes in the margins will help you keep track of the important ideas in a text. Use the *wh-* questions to decide what is most important in the paragraph.

Write notes in the margin next to the paragraphs from the reading. The first paragraph is done as an example. Use the *wh-* words as a guide.

In most Hollywood movies, the Native American Navajos still fight on horses in the American Southwest. But during World War II, a group of Navajos made their language into a weapon to protect the United States. They were the Navajo Code Talkers, and theirs is one of the few unbroken codes in military history.

WHAT?
Navajos, not only in movies
Navajo language, weapon in WW II
unbroken military code

Navajo was the perfect choice for a secret language. It is very **complex**. One vowel can have up to 10 different pronunciations, changing the meaning of any word. In the 1940s, Navajo was an unwritten language. No one outside of the reservation could speak it or understand it.

WHY?

The Navajo Code team had to invent new words to describe military equipment. For example, they named ships after fish: *lotso-whale* (battleship), *calo-shark* (destroyer), and *beshloiron-fish* (submarine). When a Code Talker received a message via radio, he heard a series of unrelated Navajo words. He would then translate the words into English and use the first letter of each English word to spell the message. The Navajo words *tsah* (needle), *wol-la-chee* (ant), *ah-kh-di-glini* (victor), and *tsah-ah-dzoh* (yucca) spelled *NAVY*.

HOW?

CRITICAL THINKING

Discuss the questions in a small group. Be prepared to share your ideas with the class.

1. "Code Talkers just said: 'I was a radioman.'" Why did they say this after the war?

2. "They named ships after fish." What does it tell you about Navajo values?

3. Do you think today's technology would make it easier to break the Navajo Code?

READING TWO: Languages Die Out, Taking History Along

A **Warm-Up**

> ***Die out*** means "to disappear or stop existing completely." Throughout history many kinds of animals have died out. For example, dinosaurs died out 65 million years ago.

Check (✓) each possible answer.

If a language is dying out, this might mean . . .

☐ the language is changing.

☐ not as many people speak it anymore.

☐ the culture in which it is spoken is disappearing.

☐ more people are speaking shared languages.

Scientists have theories about why the dinosaurs died out, but no one knows for sure.

Understanding Introductions

An **introduction** is the first paragraph of a text. After reading the introduction, the reader usually knows how the text will be organized. There are typically <u>three</u> parts in an introduction.
- The introduction often begins with one or two sentences to get the reader's attention. This is called a **hook**.
- Next, there are a few sentences that provide **background information** about the topic of the text.
- At the end of the introduction, the author usually states the focus of the text in a sentence. This is called a **thesis statement**.

1 **Read the first paragraph of the reading. Put brackets [ ] around the sentences that represent each part of the introduction.**

Kuna. Klctza. Cúu, ma chin áaje. There are many ways to say goodbye in Mam. But soon the world may be saying farewell to the Mayan language and the culture in which it **originated**. Along with Mam, the United Nations **estimates** half of the world's 6,000 languages will disappear in less than a century, while half of the world's people now use one of just eight languages: Chinese, English, Hindi, Spanish, Russian, Arabic, Portuguese, and French. Many linguists are scrambling to save dying languages, while others say it is simply the natural **evolution** of languages to continually develop, change and die off, just like species of plants and animals. In either case, the **globalization** of language is changing the culture of the world.

A Mayan drummer performs a ritual in Quintana Roo, Mexico.

2 **Discuss these questions with a partner.**

1. After reading the introduction, do you think the author will present one opinion or two opinions about languages dying out?

2. Which sentences helped you decide on your answer to question 1?

3. Which key words in those sentences helped you answer question 2?

Now read the text to get more information about disappearing languages.

Languages Die Out, Taking History Along

By Brittany Karford *Daily Universe Staff Reporter* – 16 Mar 2005
(Brigham Young University. Universe.byu.edu)

Até logo 再見 Adiós

Do widzenia **Orevwa** さようなら

1   Kuna. Klctza. Cúu, ma chin áaje. There are many ways to say goodbye in Mam. But soon the world may be saying farewell to the Mayan language and the culture in which it **originated**. Along with Mam, the United Nations **estimates** half of the world's 6,000 languages will disappear in less than a century, while half of the world's people now use one of just eight languages: Chinese, English, Hindi, Spanish, Russian, Arabic, Portuguese, and French. Many linguists are scrambling[1] to save dying languages, while others say it is simply the natural **evolution** of languages to continually develop, change, and die off, just like species of plants and animals. In either case, the **globalization** of language is changing the culture of the world.

2   Lyle Campbell is involved in language revitalization[2] because he thinks the **wisdom** of the world is encoded in its languages. He is closely involved in the **preservation** of many Mayan and Native American Indian languages, but documenting a language is a **massive** undertaking[3]. A speaker of 52 different languages,

David Stewart said once a language is lost, the culture behind it is also lost. Stewart said every language contains a **value** system and a way of thinking. While German is one of the best languages for a mechanical process, he said it would be poor in describing a walk through a forest. But, Portuguese, though clumsy[4] in speaking of a mechanical process, is quite beautiful in describing scenery.[5]

3   Ray Clifford, the director of the Center for Language Studies at BYU, is not **alarmed**. As language is constantly evolving, Clifford said even the English language of today would not be readily recognized by Shakespeare. To Clifford, the number of languages in existence today is **evidence** of man's creativity. Despite fewer languages, the people of the world are increasing their ability to communicate across groups. "The goal of world peace will never be achieved without **mutual** understanding," Clifford said. "You cannot achieve mutual understanding without effective communication, which shared language can provide." There is another way to say goodbye in the Mayan language of Mam— Q'onk chipena. It means "strength to all."

---

[1] *scrambling:* trying to do something difficult very quickly

[2] *revitalization:* the process of making something strong, active, or powerful again

[3] *undertaking:* an important job or piece of work

---

[4] *clumsy:* awkward

[5] *scenery:* the natural features of a place such as mountains and forests

COMPREHENSION

 Main Ideas

Complete each sentence with the correct word or phrase from the box.

believes	decreasing	language	not as many	shared	worried about

1. The number of languages spoken around the world is

    _____, but the number of people who speak the same

    languages is increasing.

2. Some linguists are _____ languages disappearing.

3. According to David Stewart, what a group of people

    _____ and how they think are important parts of each

    language.

4. Ray Clifford believes that _____ is always changing

    and this is natural.

5. According to Clifford, even though there are _____

    different languages today as in the past, communication between people

    from different cultures is increasing worldwide.

6. Clifford suggests that successful communication is based on

    _____ understanding, and this is very important for

    world peace.

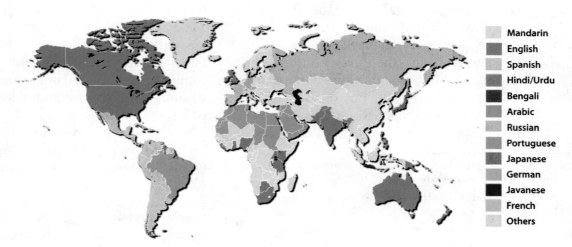

Languages spoken around the world

B **Close Reading**

Find each word, phrase, or number on the left in the reading. Then match each with the correct explanation on the right.

_____ 1. half of the world's languages *(paragraph 1)*

_____ 2. less than a century *(paragraph 1)*

_____ 3. eight *(paragraph 1)*

_____ 4. Mayan and Native American Indian languages *(paragraph 2)*

_____ 5. 52 *(paragraph 2)*

_____ 6. German *(paragraph 2)*

_____ 7. shared language *(paragraph 3)*

a. a language that describes a mechanical process well

b. the number of languages that will disappear in less than a century

c. an important part of effective communication

d. the amount of time it will take for half the world's languages to disappear

e. the languages Campell is trying to save

f. the number of languages David Stewart speaks

g. the number of languages half the world's population uses

VOCABULARY

 Suffixes

> A **suffix** is a group of letters added to the end of a word that changes the word's meaning. Recognizing **suffixes** at the end of words can help you figure out the meanings of words. For example, the suffixes *-ence*, *-dom*, *-ist*, *-sion*, and *-tion* make a word a noun. Suffixes have meanings, too. For example, *-dom* means "the place or state of being." You might know the adjective *free* but may be confused when you see *freedom*, the noun form. If you know what the suffix *-dom* means, you can figure out that *freedom* means "the state of being free."

1 **Underline the suffixes in these words.**

a. globalization

b. preservation

c. wisdom

d. evidence

e. evolution

2 **Read the definitions.**

global *(adjective)* = affecting or including the whole world

preserve *(verb)* = to keep something from being harmed, destroyed, or changed too much

wise *(adjective)* = based on good judgment or experience

evident *(adjective)* = easily noticed or understood

evolve *(verb)* = to develop and change gradually over a long period of time

3 **Decide if the sentence needs a noun, an adjective, or a verb. Circle the correct word form to complete the sentences.**

a. Chinese is becoming a **global/globalization** language.

b. Some linguists feel the **preserve/preservation** of languages is extremely important.

c. The linguists who are working hard to save dying languages feel that there is **wise/wisdom** in each language and this will be lost if the languages are not saved.

d. It is **evident/evidence** that English is becoming more and more of a shared language around the world.

e. Languages **evolve/evolution** over time. That means, the way a language was spoken in the past is not exactly the same as the way it is spoken today.

B Synonyms

Two of the words in parentheses make sense in the sentence. Cross out the word that is NOT a synonym (word with the same meaning). Check your answers with a partner.

1. Some linguists are (excited, worried, alarmed) that so many languages are disappearing.

2. Researchers (calculate, know, estimate) that 50% of the world's 6,000 languages will disappear in less than a century.

3. Many English words (ended, originated, came) from other languages.

4. (Separate, Shared, Mutual) comprehension of a language makes it possible for people around the world to communicate more easily.

C Using the Dictionary

For some words, there is more than one meaning in the dictionary. You must choose the correct meaning for the context. For example, the words *massive* and *value* have the following meanings:

> **massive** *adjective* **1** very large, solid, and heavy **2** unusually large, powerful, or damaging
>
> **value** *noun* **1** the amount of money that something is worth **2** the importance or usefulness of something **3** your beliefs about what is right or wrong

Now read each sentence. Decide which meaning is being used. Write the number of the appropriate meaning.

_____ 1. He is closely involved in the preservation of many Mayan and Native American Indian languages, but documenting a language is a **massive** undertaking.

_____ 2. A speaker of 52 different languages, David Stewart said once a language is lost, the culture behind it is also lost. Stewart said every language contains a **value** system and a way of thinking.

CRITICAL THINKING

Discuss the questions in a small group. Be prepared to share your answers with the class. Use the vocabulary you studied in the reading.

1. In the last sentence of paragraph 1, the author states that "the globalization of language is changing the culture of the world." Do you think she is expressing her personal opinion or presenting a fact?

2. Does the author present both opinions about this topic equally, or does she seem to be in favor of one side of the issue? Explain the reason for your answer.

3. Why do you think the number of languages spoken around the world is decreasing, but the number of people who speak the same languages is increasing?

4. After reading this article, do you think all languages need to be saved? Give examples from the reading to support your point of view.

AFTER YOU READ

WRITING ACTIVITY

Choose one question and write a paragraph to answer it. Use at least five of the words and phrases you studied in the chapter (for a complete list, go to page 49).

1. Why was the Navajo language so useful as a secret code?

2. How can the beliefs of a culture be saved when the language is dying out? What can people do to be sure their values do not die out with their language?

DISCUSSION AND WRITING TOPICS

Discuss these topics in a small group. Choose one of them and write a paragraph or two about it. Use the vocabulary from the chapter.

1. Why is it important to keep a secret? Have you ever had to keep a secret? How did you feel? Did you ever tell?

2. What are the benefits of knowing another language? How does knowing another language make life better for an individual as well as a group of people?

VOCABULARY

Nouns	Verbs	Adjectives	Preposition
evidence *	capture	alarmed	via*
evolution	describe	complex*	
globalization*	estimate*	massive	
preservation	memorize	mutual*	
value	mention		
wisdom	originate		
	remain		

* = AWL (Academic Word List) item

SELF-ASSESSMENT

In this chapter you learned to:

○ Scan a text for numbers

○ Read a chart for information

○ Identify the parts of an introduction

○ Understand and use synonyms

○ Understand prefixes and suffixes

○ Use a dictionary to find the meaning of vocabulary in context

○ Take margin notes to remember the main ideas

What can you do well? ☑

What do you need to practice more? ☑

CHAPTER 4

ANIMAL BEHAVIOR:
Elephants

ANIMAL BEHAVIOR: the scientific study of how animals interact with each other, with other living beings, and with the environment. It explores how animals relate to their physical environment as well as to other organisms.

OBJECTIVES

To read academic texts, you need to master certain skills.

In this chapter, you will:

- Skim a text and identify key words to figure out the main idea

- Guess the meaning of words from the context

- Understand and use synonyms

- Identify word forms from location in the sentence

- Learn word forms of new vocabulary

- Use new vocabulary to complete sentences

- Underline key words to determine the main idea

Consider This Chart

Complete the chart about what you know, what you think you know, and what you want to find out about elephants. Share your ideas in a small group.

I KNOW ELEPHANTS . . .	I THINK ELEPHANTS . . .	I'D LIKE TO FIND OUT ABOUT ELEPHANTS . . .

READING ONE: The Elephant Orphanage

A Warm-Up

Look at the list of what children need as they grow up. Check (✓) the two items that you think are the most important. Then share your answers with the class.

☐ food, clothes, shelter

☐ education

☐ love

☐ playtime

☐ rules

B Reading Strategy

Skimming

Reading something quickly to find the main idea or important facts is called **skimming**. To **skim**, read as fast as you can without stopping.

Skim the reading to find out what the elephant orphanage is. Then circle the correct words to complete the sentence.

The elephant orphanage is a place where **baby/older** elephants that **are sick/ don't have parents** live.

Now read the text to find out more about this orphanage.

The Elephant Orphanage

By Daniel Schorn

April 6, 2009

1   Stories about an orphanage are bound to pull at your heartstrings. All these orphans are from East Africa. They were all **abandoned** when they were very young, less than two years old — and they're all elephants. This orphanage is in Kenya, near Nairobi, and has been around almost 30 years.

2   Each orphan has a private room. There is a communal[1] bath, a playground, and a dining area. There are as many as 14 orphans here at any one time, and they stay a number of years before going back to the bush.[2]

3   Just about the best people you've ever met are the **gentle** men who work here. They are called keepers, and they have **extraordinary** jobs. There is one keeper per elephant; he spends 24 hours a day with his charge, seven days a week. A keeper feeds his elephant every three hours, day and night, just like mom would. He keeps his elephant warm, not like mom would, but with a blanket. He even sleeps right next to his elephant. The keepers are **rotated** now and then so that no elephant gets too **attached** to any one of them.

4   The keepers also teach the elephants how to be elephants. There are **wild** elephant things these kids don't know how to do — mother wasn't around to teach them. Things like covering themselves in dust[3] to prevent sunburn. The keepers do it with shovels,[4] until the elephants **pick it up** themselves. It's actually a pretty **lush** life for the young elephants at the orphanage. But it's not the life of a wild elephant.

5   So like any good school, this place prepares its young charges to leave. But not right away. You don't go straight from a nursery to the jungle. You need more schooling first. Therefore, the orphanage **runs** a sort of junior high school in Tsavo National Park, the biggest park in Kenya. In the park, there is a lot less **supervision** and a lot less milk. The elephants find most of their food themselves. There is no longer any concern about their survival. They are healthy and strong now. Not only that, they hang out with elephants in the wild. They're in the process of becoming wild. One day, each elephant just wanders off into the wild and stays there. It is not at the **prompting** of anyone in the orphanage. It is whenever an elephant feels that he is ready to go back where he belongs.

---

[1] *communal:* shared by a group

[2] *the bush:* wild country in Australia and Africa that has not been cleared

[3] *dust:* dry powder that consists of small pieces of dirt

[4] *shovels:* tools with a long handle used for digging or moving earth

COMPREHENSION

A Main Ideas

Write the number of the paragraph that matches each main idea from the reading.

Paragraph _____ describes what the elephants learn at the orphanage.

Paragraph _____ describes the elephants' living conditions.

Paragraph _____ is about the people who take care of the elephants.

Paragraph _____ gives general information about the orphans and orphanage.

Paragraph _____ explains how the orphanage prepares the elephants to return to their natural environment.

B Close Reading

Complete each sentence with the correct word or phrase from the box. One word will not be used.

about	get along with	one	protected
decide	less	own	survive

1. The elephants became orphans when they were _____ than two years old.

2. The elephant orphanage began _____ 30 years ago.

3. The elephants have their _____ rooms.

4. Each keeper is in charge of _____ elephant and is like a mother to that elephant.

5. The elephants learn how to _____ other elephants and

   how to _____ in the wild.

6. The elephants live in a _____ area of a national park before returning to the wild.

7. The elephants _____ when they are ready to go back to their natural environment.

VOCABULARY

A **Parts of Speech**

Look at the words in bold in the reading and decide if they are nouns (words that describe **people, places, things, qualities, actions, or ideas**), verbs (words that describe **actions, experiences, or states**), or adjectives (**words that describe nouns or pronouns**). Write the part of speech on the line next to each word.

_____verb_____ 1. abandoned   _____ 6. pick (it) up

_____ 2. extraordinary   _____ 7. runs

_____ 3. rotated   _____ 8. lush

_____ 4. attached   _____ 9. supervision

_____ 5. wild

B **Definitions**

Find each word or phrase in the reading and match it with its definition.

_c_ 1. **abandoned**   a. learn something

___ 2. **extraordinary**   b. operates

___ 3. **lush**   c. not being taken care of anymore

___ 4. **prompting**   d. very unusual or special

___ 5. **wild**   e. untamed

___ 6. **pick (it) up**   f. suggestion; urging

___ 7. **runs**   g. luxurious

C **Synonyms**

Read each sentence from the text and circle the word or phrase in parentheses that is a synonym (word with the same meaning) for the underlined word(s).

1. The keepers <u>are **rotated**</u> (**take different days off/ take care of different elephants**) now and then so that no elephant **gets** too **attached** <u>to any one of them</u> (**close to other elephants/close to one of the keepers**).

2. In the park, there is a lot less **supervision** (**protection/work**) and a lot less milk.

3. One day, each elephant just wanders off into the wild and stays there. <u>It is not at the **prompting** of anyone in the orphanage</u> (**The elephants decide to leave when they are ready/The elephants are forced to leave**).

CRITICAL THINKING

Discuss the questions in a small group. Be prepared to share your answers with the class. Use the vocabulary you studied in the reading.

1. Why do you think the author states how old the animals are when they are taken to the orphanage and how long the orphanage has existed?

2. Junior high school is usually called middle school in the United States. After finishing elementary school at the age of 11, children spend three years in middle school before going to high school. According to the reading, elephants also go to junior high school before returning to the wild. How is this stage different from the earlier stage at the orphanage?

3. The elephants decide when they want to return to their natural environment. Do you think this is a good idea? Why or why not?

READING TWO: Elephant Behavior

Ⓐ Warm-Up

Look at this photo. List the ways you think elephants use their trunks. Complete the sentence. Begin each line with a verb. Then discuss your list with a partner.

← trunk

Elephants use their trunks to:

- _____
- _____
- _____

Identifying Key Words and Phrases

The topic sentence is usually the first sentence of a paragraph. It tells the reader the main idea of the paragraph. You do not have to understand every word in the topic sentence to get the main idea. **Key words or phrases** in the topic sentence can help you figure out the main idea.

Underline the key words or phrases in the topic sentence of each paragraph in the reading. Try not to underline more than three words in each topic sentence. Share your answers with the class.

EXAMPLE: PARAGRAPH 1
<u>Young</u> elephants are raised within a <u>matriarchal</u> family, beginning with their <u>mother</u> and then including sisters, cousins, aunts, grandmothers, and friends.

Now read the article to learn more about elephants.

Elephant Behavior

By Charles Siebert
National Geographic, September 2011

1   Young elephants are **raised** within a matriarchal[1] family, beginning with their mother and then including sisters, cousins, aunts, grandmothers, and friends. These **bonds** endure over a lifetime that can be as long as 70 years. Young elephants stay close to their mothers and **extended family** members—males until they are about 14, females for life. According to Daphne Sheldrick, founder and director of an elephant orphanage in Kenya for over 30 years, "Whenever we get a new baby here, the others will come around and lovingly put their trunks on its back to comfort it. They have such big hearts."

---

[1] *matriarchal:* having a family or social group in which the females have the most influence and power

2   A **complex** communication system helps the elephants stay connected. Elephants express emotions using their trunk, ears, head, and tail. When they need to communicate over longer distances, they use powerful low-frequency, rumbling calls[2] that can be heard by others more than a mile away.

3   After a death, family members show signs of **grief**. Field biologists such as Joyce Poole, who has studied Africa's elephants for more than 35 years, describe elephants trying to lift the dead body and covering it with dirt and brush.[3] Poole once watched a female stand guard over her stillborn[4] baby for three days, her head, ears, and trunk hanging in grief. Elephants may revisit the bones of the **deceased** for months, even years, touching them with their trunks and creating paths to visit the carcass.[5]

4   "Elephants are very human animals," says Sheldrick. "Their emotions are exactly the same as ours." Studies show that elephant brains are very similar to those in humans in the way they **process** emotions. The elephant brain also has a large quantity of spindle cells, which are thought to be related to **empathy** and social awareness in humans. Elephants have even passed the mirror test of self-recognition, something only humans, and some great apes and dolphins, had been known to do.

---

[2] ***low-frequency, rumbling calls:*** infrasound used by elephants to communicate over long distances; sounds that the human ear cannot hear

[3] ***brush:*** small bushes and trees covering an open area of land

[4] ***stand guard over her stillborn:*** stay with and watch a baby that is born dead

[5] ***carcass:*** the body of a dead animal

COMPREHENSION

A Main Ideas

Check (✓) each possible answer.

This reading is about how elephants . . .

☐ form relationships.

☐ differ if they are male or female.

☐ hunt for food.

☐ communicate.

☐ express feelings.

☐ protect themselves.

☐ are similar to people.

B Close Reading

Read each statement. Decide if it is *True* or *False* according to the reading. Check (✓) the appropriate box. If it is false, change it to make it true. Discuss your answers with a partner.

	TRUE	FALSE
1. Female elephants play the most important role in the family.	☐	☐
2. Male elephants separate from their female relatives before they are 14.	☐	☐
3. Elephants communicate only by making sounds.	☐	☐
4. Elephants feel sad for a long time after another elephant dies.	☐	☐
5. Elephants handle their feelings in some of the same ways people do.	☐	☐
6. If elephants look in a mirror, they do not know they are looking at themselves.	☐	☐

VOCABULARY

A Synonyms

Find each word or phrase on the left in the reading and match it with its synonym(s), or word(s) with the same meaning, on the right.

__f__ 1. **raised**   **a.** relationships

____ 2. **bonds**   **b.** deal with

____ 3. **extended family**   **c.** sadness, pain

____ 4. **complex**   **d.** understanding, compassion

____ 5. **grief**   **e.** dead

____ 6. **deceased**   **f.** educated

____ 7. **process**   **g.** aunts, uncles, and cousins

____ 8. **empathy**   **h.** intricate (not simple)

B Word Forms

Choose the correct word forms from the chart to complete the sentences.
An *X* indicates there is no form in that category.

	NOUN	VERB	ADJECTIVE
1.	complexity	X	complex
2.	grief	grieve	X
3.	empathy	X	empathetic
4.	process	process	X
5.	bond	bond	X

1. complexity, complex

   The way elephants communicate is very _____.

   The _____ of how elephants express emotions is fascinating.

2. grief, grieve

   Elephants _____ for a long time after another elephant dies.

   Elephants feel deep _____ after the death of another elephant.

3. empathy, empathetic

   Elephants are _____ because they are able to understand other elephants' emotions.

   The similarity between elephant and human brains might explain why

   elephants, like humans, show _____.

4. process *(verb)*, process *(noun)*

   Taking care of orphaned elephants is a difficult _____.

   Elephants are similar to people in the way that they _____ feelings.

5. bond *(verb)*, bond *(noun)*

   Elephants at the orphanage have a very close _____ to the keepers who take care of them.

   Baby elephants _____ with their mothers.

ⓒ Word Usage

Complete the sentences with the correct word(s) from the box. Use each word only once. Not all the words will be used.

bonds	deceased	extended family	process
complex	empathetic	grieve	

1. The _____ bonds _____ between female elephants last a lifetime.

2. Young elephants grow up with their _____.

3. Elephants are _____ and sometimes use their trunks to hug other elephants that are sad or lonely.

4. Elephants use a _____ system to communicate.

5. Elephants watch over their _____ for long periods of time.

6. People and elephants _____ feelings in the same way because of the similarity of their brains.

NOTE-TAKING: Underlining Key Words

Go back to the reading and read it again. Underline the key words that describe elephant behavior. Look at the words you underlined and choose the answer that best completes the following sentence.

Overall, this passage is about . . .

a. the physical characteristics of elephants.

b. the emotions of elephants.

c. the relationship between elephants and their physical environment.

CRITICAL THINKING

Discuss the questions in a small group. Be prepared to share your answers with the class. Use the vocabulary you studied in the reading.

1. How are baby elephants similar to human babies?

2. How do you think scientists were able to figure out elephants' complex communication system?

3. How do scientists know elephants recognize themselves in a mirror?

4. Why do you think some animals show signs of grief and others do not?

AFTER YOU READ

WRITING ACTIVITY

With a partner, write an interview between a newspaper reporter and Daphne Sheldrick, founder and director of an elephant orphanage in Kenya for more than 30 years. Use at least five facts from the readings in your interview. Also use some of the words you studied in the chapter (for a complete list, go to page 62).

DISCUSSION AND WRITING TOPICS

Discuss these topics in a small group. Choose one of them and write a paragraph or two about it. Use the vocabulary from the chapter.

1. The elephant orphanage described in Reading One is an organization that is supported by donations. Would you give money to support this cause? Why or why not?

2. The first sentence in Reading One reads: "Stories about an orphanage are bound to pull at your heartstrings." This expression means that something causes strong feelings of compassion. Discuss two pieces of information from the readings that pulled at your heartstrings.

VOCABULARY

Nouns	Verbs	Adjectives	Phrases and Idioms
bonds*	abandon*	attached	pick (it) up
deceased	process*	complex*	
empathy	raise	extraordinary	
extended family	rotate	lush	
grief	run	wild	
prompting			
supervision			

* = AWL (Academic Word List) item

SELF-ASSESSMENT

In this chapter you learned to:

- ○ Skim a text and identify key words to figure out the main idea
- ○ Guess the meaning of words from the context
- ○ Understand and use synonyms
- ○ Identify word forms from location in the sentence
- ○ Learn word forms of new vocabulary
- ○ Use new vocabulary to complete sentences
- ○ Underline key words to determine the main idea

What can you do well? ☑

What do you need to practice more? ☑

CHAPTER 5

SOCIAL PSYCHOLOGY:
Teaching Tolerance

SOCIAL PSYCHOLOGY: the branch of psychology that studies people and their relationships with other people, with groups, and with society as a whole

OBJECTIVES

To read academic texts, you need to master certain skills.

In this chapter, you will:

- Predict the content of a text by using visuals

- Determine whether a word has a positive or negative meaning

- Understand and use antonyms

- Use a synopsis to understand the main ideas of a passage

- Understand the meaning of new words based on the context

- Use a dictionary to determine the correct definition of a word

- Identify word forms of new vocabulary

- Sort important details in a text

Consider These Facts

Discuss the ideas in a small group.

1. Dr. Martin Luther King, Jr., was an outstanding leader in the civil rights movement in the United States from 1955 to 1968. What do you know about him? Make a list.

2. Dr. King said, "The time is always right to do what is right." Explain what you think this means.

READING ONE: A Class Divided—Jane Elliott's Famous Lesson

A Warm-Up

Look at the painting and consider these questions. Discuss the questions with a partner.

1. What do you see in this painting?

2. Where and when do you think it takes place?

3. How does it make you feel?

B Reading Strategy

Predicting Content from Visuals

Predicting is a very important pre-reading skill. When you **predict**, you make a guess about something based on the information you have. Predicting helps prepare the reader for the reading experience that is to come. Pictures in a text can often help you predict what the text is about.

Look at the photo in the reading. The children with the collars have been separated from the others. Check (✓) all the possible ways that the teacher Jane Elliott could have divided her class based on what you see in the photo.

Jane Elliott could have divided her class into two groups by . . .

☐ gender   ☐ skin color

☐ height   ☐ religion

☐ intelligence   ☐ eye color

Now read the text to learn about this lesson.

A CLASS DIVIDED—JANE ELLIOTT'S FAMOUS LESSON

1   On the day after Martin Luther King Jr. was **murdered** in April 1968, Jane Elliott's third-graders from the small, all-white town of Riceville, Iowa, came to class confused and upset. They recently had made King their "Hero of the Month," and they couldn't understand why someone would kill him. So Elliott decided to teach her class a **daring** lesson in the meaning of discrimination.[1] She wanted to show her pupils what discrimination feels like, and what it can do to people.

2   Elliott divided her class by eye color—those with blue eyes and those with brown. On the first day, the blue-eyed children were told they were smarter, nicer, neater,[2] and better than those with brown eyes. Throughout the day, Elliott praised[3] them and allowed them **privileges** such as taking a longer recess[4] and being first in the lunch line. **In contrast**, the brown-eyed children had to wear collars around their necks, and their behavior and performance were criticized by Elliott. On the second day, the roles were **reversed**, and the blue-eyed children were made to feel **inferior**.

(continued on next page)

---

[1] *discrimination:* the practice of treating one group of people differently from another in an unfair way

[2] *neater:* more organized

[3] *praised:* said publicly that someone has done something well

[4] *recess:* a time when children are allowed to go outside to play during the school day

3 What happened over the course of the **unique** two-day exercise **astonished** both students and teacher. On both days, children who were assigned to the inferior group took on the look and behavior of inferior students, performing poorly on tests and other work. In contrast, the "superior" students—students who had been sweet and **tolerant** before the exercise—became mean-spirited[5] and seemed to like discriminating against the "inferior" group.

4 "I watched what had been marvelous, cooperative, wonderful,

_____

[5] *mean-spirited:* angry and unpleasant

thoughtful children turn into nasty,[6] **vicious**, discriminating little third-graders in a space of 15 minutes," says Elliott. She says she realized then that she had "created a microcosm[7] of society in a third-grade classroom."

5 Elliott said that after this exercise, when the pain was over and they were all back together, that the kids said they felt like a family. "They found out how to hurt one another and they found out how it feels to be hurt in that way and they refused to hurt one another in that way again."

_____

[6] *nasty:* very mean, cruel

[7] *microcosm:* a miniature copy of something

COMPREHENSION

A Main Ideas

Circle the correct answer.

1. Elliott's third-graders **knew/didn't know** a lot about Dr. Martin Luther King, Jr.

2. Elliott decided to have her class **read about/experience** discrimination.

3. Elliott's lesson lasted two **days/weeks**.

4. The children **wearing/not wearing** the collars were treated badly.

5. The third-graders **usually/seldom** behaved in a positive way before the lesson.

6. The children **learned/didn't learn** how it felt to cause and experience pain.

B Close Reading

Complete the sentences by matching the two columns. Compare answers with a partner.

_____ 1. The children wearing the collars

_____ 2. The children <u>not</u> wearing the collars

_____ 3. The collars made the children

_____ 4. The children's behavior

_____ 5. The children felt

a. got more time to play.

b. feel less intelligent.

c. like a family again after the lesson.

d. were treated unfairly by Elliott.

e. changed very fast.

VOCABULARY

A Connotations

Some words have **feelings** connected to them depending on how they are used in a sentence. These feelings, or **connotations**, can be **positive** (good or useful) or **negative** (bad or harmful).

Look at each word. Find the word in the reading. Decide whether it has a *Positive* or *Negative* meaning. Check the appropriate box. Discuss your answers with a partner.

	POSITIVE	NEGATIVE
1. murdered	☐	☐
2. privileges	☐	☐
3. tolerant	☐	☐
4. vicious	☐	☐

B Antonyms

An **antonym** is a word that has the opposite meaning of another word.

Go back to the reading. Find the bold words that mean the opposite.

1. _____ ≠ also (*paragraph 2*)

2. _____ ≠ kept the same (*paragraph 2*)

3. _____ ≠ superior (*paragraph 3*)

Complete the paragraph with the correct word.

> **astonished** *verb* surprised
>
> **daring** *adjective* willing to do dangerous or difficult things; brave
>
> **thoughtful** *adjective* considerate, kind

Jane Elliott is a brave woman who took a big risk with her third-grade students almost 50 years ago. Her _____ exercise
1.
changed her students' understanding of discrimination. The immediate change in the students' behavior _____ both Elliott
2.
and her students. For example, before the lesson the children were very

_____ and caring, but during the lesson those who were
3.
not wearing collars became very inconsiderate. However, they were taught a unique lesson because they all felt the pain of feeling inferior.

NOTE-TAKING: Sorting Information

> When a reading describes two different ideas, events, or people, you can take notes on the key words or phrases that represent each side. For instance, you could circle the words or phrases for one side and underline those for the other. Then you can put the information in a chart to organize the main points of the text.

Sort the notes below by putting them into the correct column in the chart on the next page. Go back to the reading to check the information if you do not remember.

- became mean-spirited
- behavior and performance criticized by Elliott
- given privileges: longer recess, first in lunch line
- made to feel inferior
- performed badly on tests and other work
- seemed to like discriminating against the other group
- told that they were nicer, smarter, neater, better
- turned into nasty, vicious, discriminating children in 15 minutes

SUPERIOR GROUP	INFERIOR GROUP

CRITICAL THINKING

Discuss the questions in a small group. Be prepared to share your answers with the class. Use the vocabulary you studied in the reading.

1. What adjectives are used in paragraph 1 to describe the town of Riceville, Iowa? Why are these words important?

2. Elliott's lesson was conducted over two days. Why do you think she didn't continue it for a longer period of time?

3. In paragraph 4, Elliott's classroom is described as "a microcosm of society." What do you think this means? Why is this important?

READING TWO: Fourteen Years Later

 Warm-Up

Discuss the question with a partner. Give reasons to support your opinion.

Imagine you are a parent of a third-grader (an eight- or nine-year-old). Would you let your child participate in Jane Elliott's lesson?

Understanding a Synopsis

A **synopsis** is a short description of the most important information in a reading. This description gives the reader a brief summary of the text.

Read the synopsis at the beginning of the reading. Then fill in the chart. Put a question mark (?) in the chart if information answering the question is not given in the synopsis.

WHO?	WHEN?	WHERE?	WHAT?	HOW OR WHY?

Now read the transcript to find out more about what the students remember.

Fourteen Years Later

1 Fourteen years after Jane Elliott did her exercise for the third time, FRONTLINE's "A Class Divided" broadcasted a mini-**reunion** of that 1970 third-grade class. As young adults, Elliott's **former** students watched themselves on film and talked about the **impact** Elliott's lesson in discrimination has had on their lives and attitudes.

2 **CHARLIE COBB:** The reunion of her former third-graders was Jane Elliott's first chance to find out how much of her lesson her students had remembered.

3 **JANE ELLIOTT:** Raymond. Why—I want to know why . . . you . . . were so **eager** to discriminate against the rest of these kids.

RAYMOND: It felt tremendously evil.[1] All your inhibitions[2] were gone. It didn't matter if they were my friends or not, you had a chance to get all your anger out on anyone who had caused you pain.

---

[1] *evil:* very bad and harmful

[2] *inhibitions:* feelings of worry or embarrassment that stop you from expressing how you really feel or doing what you really want to do

4 **JANE ELLIOTT:**	How did you feel when you were in the out-group[3]?
VERLA:	That day, after we went home — (laughs), oooh, you know, talk about hating somebody.
WOMAN:	Yeah.
JANE ELLIOTT:	You hated me.
VERLA:	Yeah. Nobody likes to be looked down upon. Nobody likes to be hated, **teased**, or discriminated against. You just get so mad.
5 **JANE ELLIOTT:**	Were you just angry, or was there more than that?
RAYMOND:	I felt demoralized,[4] **humiliated**.
6 **JANE ELLIOTT:**	Is the learning worth the **agony**?
EVERYONE:	Yes.
JANE ELLIOTT:	Should every—should every child have the exercise or should every teacher?
EVERYBODY:	Everybody.
RAYMOND:	Every school ought to implement[5] something like this program in their early stages of education.
7 **CHARLIE COBB:**	If Jane Elliott's lesson in discrimination changed the way these young people feel about discrimination and racism, it also had a totally **unexpected** result.
JANE ELLIOTT:	The second year I did this exercise I gave little spelling tests, math tests, reading tests two weeks before the exercise, each day of the exercise, and two weeks later, and, almost without exception, the students' scores go up on the day they're on the top, down the day they're on the bottom, and then maintain a higher level for the rest of the year, after they've been through the exercise. We sent some of those tests to Stanford University to the Psychology Department, and they did, sort of an informal review of them, and they said that what's happening here is kids' academic ability is being changed in a 24-hour period. And it isn't possible, but it's happening. Something very strange is happening to these children because suddenly they're finding out how really great they are and they are responding to what they know now they are able to do. And it's happened **consistently** with third-graders.

[3] *out-group:* the inferior group

[4] *demoralized:* hopeless

[5] *implement:* to begin to make a plan or process happen

COMPREHENSION

A **Main Ideas**

Check (✓) the feelings that Elliott's 1970 third-graders who are now adults discuss in the reading.

At the time of the lesson, the students felt

☐ angry

☐ embarrassed

☐ hated

☐ hopeless

☐ jealous

☐ mad

☐ scared

B **Close Reading**

Read each statement. Decide if it is *True* or *False* according to the reading. Check (✓) the appropriate box. If it is false, change it to make it true.

	TRUE	FALSE
1. Jane Elliott wanted to find out how much her students from 14 years before remembered about the unique exercise.	☐	☐
2. On the day Raymond was in the group on the bottom, he felt he could take revenge on the kids who had hurt him earlier in the school year.	☐	☐
3. Verla hated the kids in the superior group on the day she was on the bottom.	☐	☐
4. Some members of the group felt that the exercise was valuable even though it was painful.	☐	☐
5. Elliott's former students felt students but not teachers should participate in this exercise.	☐	☐
6. Students grades improved when they were on the top.	☐	☐

VOCABULARY

A Definitions

Find each word in the reading and match it with its definition.

__d__ 1. reunion

_____ 2. former

_____ 3. eager

_____ 4. agony

_____ 5. humiliated

_____ 6. consistently

a. always in the same way or with the same attitudes or qualities

b. feeling ashamed or stupid, especially when other people are present

c. having a particular position in the past, but not now

d. a meeting of people who have not met for a long time

e. having a strong desire to do something or a strong interest in something

f. very severe pain or suffering

B Using the Dictionary

For some words, there is more than one meaning in the dictionary. You must choose the correct meaning for the context.

> **impact** *noun* **1** the effect that a person or situation has on someone or something **2** the force of one object hitting another
>
> **tease** *verb* **1** to make jokes about someone in order to annoy him/her because you think it is funny **2** to make (someone) feel excitement or interest about something you might do or say without actually doing it or saying it

Decide which meaning is being used in the reading. Write the number of the appropriate meaning.

_____ 1. As young adults, Elliott's former students watched themselves on film and talked about the **impact** Elliott's lesson in discrimination has had on their lives and attitudes. *(part 1)*

_____ 2. Nobody likes to be hated, or **teased**, or discriminated against. *(part 4)*

C Word Forms

Complete each sentence with the correct form of the word. Use a dictionary if necessary. An X indicates that there is no form in that category.

	NOUN	VERB	ADJECTIVE	ADVERB
1.	agony	agonize	agonizing	agonizingly
2.	humiliation	humiliate	humiliated/humiliating	X
3.	X	X	consistent	consistently

1. Jane Elliott's former third-graders discussed the _____ *agonizing* _____ exercise of facing discrimination.

2. When Elliott criticized the group wearing the collars, they felt

   _____.

3. Elliott's behavior was _____. She always treated the children not wearing the collars better than those who were wearing the collars.

4. The _____ of discrimination is not easily forgotten.

5. Both the children and Elliott were astonished at how easy it was for the

   group on top to _____ the group on the bottom.

6. The children who were told that they were doing great work did

   _____ better on their tests.

CRITICAL THINKING

Discuss the questions in a small group. Be prepared to share your answers with the class. Use the vocabulary you studied in the reading.

1. Charlie Cobb, the broadcaster, explains that Elliott's former third-graders watched and discussed the film of the unique exercise. Do you think they needed to watch it again? Why or why not?

2. Why are these memories so clear after such a long time?

3. How do you think this experience affects Elliott's former students now?

4. Jane Elliott's lesson was very valuable to elementary school children. In what other settings might this lesson be worthwhile?

WRITING ACTIVITY

Imagine you are one of Elliott's former third-graders who participated in her famous lesson on discrimination. Write her a letter about how you felt when you participated in the exercise, how you felt after it was over and you discussed it as a class, and how it affects your life now.

DISCUSSION AND WRITING TOPICS

Discuss these topics in a small group. Choose one of them and write a paragraph or two about it. Use the vocabulary from the chapter (for a complete list, go to page 76).

1. Where does discrimination come from? Are we born with it, or do we learn it? Give details and reasons to support your answer.

2. Do you think parents in your native country would allow their children to participate in this lesson? Why or why not?

VOCABULARY

Nouns	Verbs	Adjectives	Adverb
agony	astonished	astonished	consistently*
impact*	murdered	daring	
privileges	reversed*	eager	**Phrases and Idioms**
reunion	teased	former	in contrast
		humiliated	
		inferior	
		thoughtful	
		tolerant	
		vicious	

* = AWL (Academic Word List) item

SELF-ASSESSMENT

In this chapter you learned to:

○ Predict the content of a text by using visuals

○ Determine whether a word has a positive or negative meaning

○ Understand and use antonyms

○ Use a synopsis to understand the main ideas of a passage

○ Understand the meaning of new words based on the context

○ Use a dictionary to determine the correct definition of a word

○ Identify word forms of new vocabulary

○ Sort important details in a text

What can you do well? ☑

What do you need to practice more? ☑

CHAPTER 6

PUBLIC ART: Experiencing Familiar Places in a New Way

PUBLIC ART: Permanent or temporary physical works of art visible to the general public

OBJECTIVES

To read academic texts, you need to master certain skills.

In this chapter, you will:

- Scan texts for specific facts

- Guess the meaning of words from the context

- Understand collocations, or how words go together in English

- Identify word forms from location in the sentence

- Understand and use synonyms and antonyms

- Locate a thesis statement to understand the main idea of a text

- Use underlining to identify key words in a text

Consider These Quotes

"The work of the artist is to lift up people's hearts and help them endure."[1]

—*William Faulkner*

"Art washes away from the soul the dust of everyday life."

—*Pablo Picasso*

Circle the statement that best explains the quotes. Share your answer with a partner. Then discuss why you agree or disagree with the quotes.

Art is inspiring because artists . . .

    a. put a lot of emotion into their work.

    b. never stop trying to create their vision.

    c. give us a fresh way of seeing the world.

READING ONE: What is Public Art?

Ⓐ Warm-Up

Look at the photos on this page and at the beginning of the chapter. Discuss the questions in a small group.

1. Imagine that these works of art were temporarily placed in your town or city close to where you work or go to school. Would you enjoy looking at them? Why or why not?

2. How might this public art change your daily routine, such as commuting to work or school? Why?

[1] *endure:* to not give up

Scanning

Scanning is useful when looking for specific facts. To **scan**, quickly look over the text to find the necessary information.

Scan paragraph 1 for information to complete the sentence. Check (✓) all the possible answers.

Public art is . . .

☐ often found outside

☐ free

☐ only for adults

☐ sometimes located in nature

Now read the text to find out more about public art.

What is Public Art?

1   What is the first word that you think of when you hear the word *art*? For many people, the answer is very likely to be *museum* because we often think of art as something we see inside. However, not all art is found indoors. *Public art* is artwork that is specifically created for public spaces. It is free and **accessible** to all people. This artwork can be architecture,[1] sculpture,[2] painting, stained glass,[3] or even live performances such as concerts or dances that occur in public places. Public art can be found in **urban** centers such as pedestrian walkways, public buildings such as government offices, airports, libraries, or university or college campuses, for example. Some public artworks may be found in **rural** areas where they can be appreciated in nature. Other types of public art such

(continued on next page)

---

[1] *architecture:* the art and science of designing and constructing buildings
[2] *sculpture:* figures made from stone
[3] *stained glass:* glass that has been colored

as fireworks[4] can be viewed in the sky at night. Some public art **installations** are **permanent** and others are temporary, placed in a location for a limited amount of time.

2   Public art is a powerful and **unifying** force. Since it is located in public places, it attracts the attention of all people who are willing to slow down and really see what is around them. It can energize public spaces, transform landscapes, and invite **interaction**. Strangers may get into a conversation about a work of art, and children might ask questions about what they see. Public art has the potential to get us to look at familiar surroundings from a different **perspective**. Public art makes us think, and calms our hurried lifestyle, which might even **enhance** our quality of life.

3   Public art also has the potential to stimulate[5] economic development by increasing jobs and tourism. In 1999, Mass MoCA, one of the largest centers for contemporary art, opened. It is located on 13 acres, one-third of the downtown business district of North Adams, Massachusetts. Unused 19th-century buildings were renovated[6] to create this complex, which is so large that it includes an art gallery the size of a football field and an 850-square-foot theater. With 120,000 visitors annually, it's not difficult to see how financially **beneficial** this is for the local community.

---

[4] *fireworks:* chemicals that make loud and colorful explosions in the sky

[5] *stimulate:* to increase

[6] *renovated:* restored to good condition

COMPREHENSION

Ⓐ   Main Ideas

Complete the sentences with the correct word from the box.

economy	many	relax	settings	short

1. There are _____ types of public art.

2. Public art can be located in many _____.

3. Some public art installations can be seen only for a

   _____ period of time.

4. Public art can get people to _____, enjoy familiar surroundings, and even talk to people they don't know.

5. Public art can also help the _____ of a local community.

B Close Reading

Write each detail from the list under the appropriate heading.

- 120,000 people visit Mass MoCa
- children ask questions
- people slow down and appreciate their surroundings
- countryside, farmland
- places where people walk, government buildings, libraries, land that belongs to universities
- helps us relax
- transforms landscapes
- increases jobs

LOCATIONS FOR PUBLIC ART	ADVANTAGES OF PUBLIC ART
I. Urban Centers	**Improves Our Lives**
II. Rural Areas	**Increases Tourism**

VOCABULARY

Looking up every unfamiliar word in the dictionary is not an effective way to read. It is much better to **guess the meaning of unfamiliar words from the rest of the sentence or paragraph (the context)** and keep reading. Some words in particular can help you guess. No one guesses correctly all the time. But practice makes all the difference. You can use the dictionary after you get the main idea of the reading.

A Guessing from Context

Look at the list of words from the reading. Read the text and guess the meanings of the words from the context. Then match the words with their meanings.

_c_ 1. interaction   **a.** in a city or close to a city

____ 2. installations   **b.** available to everyone

____ 3. permanent   **c.** the activity of talking with other people

____ 4. urban   **d.** lasting for a very long time

____ 5. accessible   **e.** artwork put together by the artist

B Collocations

When **words** are **used together regularly**, they become a pair and are called **collocations**. The word pairing is not for grammatical reasons, but because of the association with each other. For example, we say "fast food" but "a quick meal."

With a partner, decide whether these words can be used together. Check (✓) *Yes* or *No*. If the words cannot be used together, go back to the reading and find the words that go together.

	YES	NO
1. permanent installation	☐	☐
2. rural centers	☐	☐
3. urban areas	☐	☐
4. unifying force	☐	☐
5. varied perspectives	☐	☐
6. quality of living	☐	☐

Antonyms

Match each word on the left with its antonym (word that has the opposite meaning). Look at the word in the reading to help you figure this out.

__c__ 1. unifying   **a.** urban

_____ 2. permanent   **b.** worsen

_____ 3. enhance   **c.** separating

_____ 4. beneficial   **d.** temporary

_____ 5. rural   **e.** harmful

NOTE-TAKING: Underlining Key Words

Go back to the reading. Underline 10 key words or phrases that would help you explain what public art is.

EXAMPLE:

What is the first word that you think of when you hear the word *art*? For many people, the answer is very likely to be *museum* because we often think of art as something we see inside. However, not all art is found indoors. *Public art* is artwork that is specifically <u>created for public spaces</u>.

CRITICAL THINKING

Discuss the questions in a small group. Be prepared to share your opinions with the class.

1. Why do you think some public art is installed only temporarily?

2. Why do you think it is more difficult today to slow down, appreciate our surroundings, and talk with one another?

3. What do you think the downtown business district of North Adams, Massachusetts, might be like if Mass MoCA had not been created?

A **Warm-Up**

Discuss the question with a partner.

If you were going to have an artist put a public art installation in your hometown, where would you have it placed? Why?

B **Reading Strategy**

Identifying a Thesis Statement

A **thesis statement** is usually found at the end of the introduction to a text, or its first paragraph. The author tells the reader the main point or the focus of the text in the thesis statement.

Underline the thesis statement in the last sentence of the first paragraph of the reading. Then check (✓) the information you think you will find in paragraphs 2, 3, and 4 of the text.

☐ The cost of each project

☐ The amount of time it took to complete each project

☐ The public's opinion of each project

☐ A description of what the artwork looked like

☐ The amount of time the public art installation was available to the public

Now read the text to see if you were correct.

Christo and Jeanne-Claude

1   Imagine a **prestigious** building in a major city wrapped like a present. How about bridges, islands, or trees **transformed** by colorful fabric that moves with the wind? You don't need to imagine this because for over 40 years Bulgarian-born Christo Javacheff and French-born Jeanne-Claude de Guillebon have been creating, designing, and installing their unusual artwork around the world. Since meeting in Paris, France, in 1957, this **energetic** husband-and-wife team who go by their first names, Christo and Jeanne-Claude, have created "'gentle disturbances'[1] in spaces . . . to make people become more aware[2] of themselves and their surroundings." This **acclaimed** couple has completed 22 unique projects that invite viewers to experience familiar environments in new ways. Each project takes many years of planning, is a temporary installation, and transforms a vast[3] urban or rural space.

_____
[1] *disturbances:* interruptions
[2] *aware:* attentive
[3] *vast:* very large

2   *The Pont-Neuf Wrapped* in Paris in 1985 is an example of the **vision** of Christo and Jeanne-Claude. After ten years of planning, the Pont Neuf, a bridge that has connected the left and right banks of the Seine River in Paris for more than 400 years, was wrapped in 454,178 square feet (40,876 square meters) of golden, silky[4] fabric by 300 professional workers. For 14 days, all surfaces of this historical bridge, as well as the lamps and sidewalks, were covered. Pedestrians could actually walk on the fabric.

3   The work of Christo and Jeanne-Claude has not only transformed historical sites in cities but has also dramatically changed natural environments. In 1991, at sunrise, *The Umbrellas* was installed. Nearly 2,000 workers opened 3,100 umbrellas in Japan and California in the United States. This public art installation spanned 12 miles (19 kilometers) in Japan and 18 miles (29 kilometers) in California. The blue umbrellas were placed close together to **represent** the limited space in Japan, while the yellow umbrellas in California were spread out in many directions, showing the vastness of the land. For 18 days, these **huge**, free-standing umbrellas became "houses without walls" and invited the public to experience nature in a new way.

4   *The Gates*, which appeared in Central Park in New York City, is an example of Christo and Jeanne-Claude's artwork in a natural environment within a major, international city. After 26 years of planning and **negotiating**, Christo and Jeanne-Claude were finally given permission to install *The Gates* in February of 2005. The 7,503 saffron[5]-colored panels were installed by 600 workers throughout the park. This "golden river" transformed the familiar footpaths and took the public on a magical journey for 16 days as the color reflected off the snow and brightened the cold, dark days of February.

5   While the journey has not been easy for Christo and Jeanne-Claude, their artwork has **touched** the public for almost half a century. And this is a key element of every project: people. The artists want their art to be in populated spaces where people can interact with it. It serves no practical purpose but is creative and beautiful. It is supposed to make people smile. While each installation is temporary, the memory of the artwork lasts a long time after it is taken down.

---

[4] *silky:* smooth and soft

[5] *saffron:* deep orange

COMPREHENSION

A **Main Ideas**

Read each statement. Decide if it is *True* or *False* according to the reading. Check (✓) the appropriate box. If it is false, change it to make it true. Discuss your answers with a partner.

	TRUE	FALSE
1. Christo and Jeanne-Claude are famous only in France.	☐	☐
2. They have completed 40 projects.	☐	☐
3. The Pont Neuf was completely covered.	☐	☐
4. *The Umbrellas* is an example of an installation in an urban setting.	☐	☐
5. *The Gates* was installed over a river in Central Park in New York City.	☐	☐
6. An important part of Christo and Jeanne-Claude's artwork is that the public can experience it in a personal way.	☐	☐

B **Close Reading**

Go back to the reading. Find the numbers that complete these details from the reading and fill in the chart.

THE PONT-NEUF WRAPPED, 1985	THE UMBRELLAS, 1991	THE GATES, 2005
____ years of planning	____ workers	____ years of planning
____ square meters of silky fabric	____ umbrellas	____ saffron-colored panels
____ workers	____ miles in Japan	____ workers
____ days	____ miles in California	____ days
	____ days	

VOCABULARY

A Word Usage

Look at the words in bold in the reading. Decide if each word describes the artists or the artwork. List the words in the chart.

Artists	Artwork
energetic	prestigious

B Word Forms

Complete the sentences with the correct form of the words.

1. energy, energize, energetic

   Christo and Jeanne-Claude needed a lot of _____
   to complete so many projects around the world.

2. negotiation, negotiate, negotiable

   Christo and Jeanne-Claude had to _____ with a lot of
   people to get permission to install their artwork.

3. representation, represent

   Because Japan is a much smaller country than the United States,
   Christo and Jeanne-Claude decided to have *The Umbrellas*

   _____ this by how close each umbrella was placed to
   the next one.

4. transformation, transform

   Christo and Jeanne-Claude's installations _____
   a wide variety of public spaces.

C Synonyms

Complete each sentence with a word from the box. Use the synonym (word with a similar meaning) in parentheses to help you select the correct word. Compare answers with a partner.

acclaimed	huge	touches	vision
gentle	prestigious	transforms	

1. There are a lot of international students at Columbia University because it

   is a very _____ prestigious _____ school.
   (respected)

2. Public art _____ familiar places for a short period
   (changes in a positive way)

   of time.

3. Christo and Jeanne-Claude are _____ for their unique
   (celebrated)

   artistic expression.

4. The fabric used by Christo and Jeanne-Claude has a

   _____ effect on the public space.
   (soft)

5. Because the installations of Christo and Jeanne-Claude are

   _____, hundreds or thousands of workers are needed
   (enormous)

   to set up each project.

6. Public art _____ us, getting us to slow down and
   (affects)

   enjoy what is around us.

7. The _____ of Christo and Jeanne-Claude has been an
   (dream)

   inspiration for almost half a century.

CRITICAL THINKING

Discuss the questions in a small group. Be prepared to share your opinions with the class.

1. Why do you think Christo and Jeanne-Claude covered the sidewalks and lamps in *The Pont-Neuf Wrapped*?

2. In Reading One, public art is described as a "unifying force." How might *The Umbrellas* and *The Gates* be examples of this?

3. Why do you think Christo and Jeanne-Claude's artwork is always temporary?

4. Should children be exposed to art in school? Should they be taught about art and how to make art?

AFTER YOU READ

WRITING ACTIVITY

Write an interview with Christo. (Jeanne-Claude died in 2009.) Include at least three pieces of information from each reading. Use at least five vocabulary words from this chapter (for a complete list, go to page 90).

DISCUSSION AND WRITING TOPICS

Discuss these topics in a small group. Choose one of them and write a paragraph or two about it. Use the vocabulary from the chapter.

1. Do you think public art benefits the community? How?

2. Do you think installing public art is a good use of money? Why or why not?

VOCABULARY

Nouns	Verbs	Adjectives
installations	enhance*	accessible*
interaction*	represent	acclaimed
negotiating	touch	beneficial*
perspective*	transform*	energetic*
vision*		gentle
		huge
		permanent
		prestigious
		rural
		unifying*
		urban

* = AWL (Academic Word List) item

SELF-ASSESSMENT

In this chapter you learned to:

- ○ Scan texts for specific facts
- ○ Guess the meaning of words from the context
- ○ Understand collocations, or how words go together in English
- ○ Identify word forms from location in the sentence
- ○ Understand and use synonyms and antonyms
- ○ Locate a thesis statement to understand the main idea of a text
- ○ Use underlining to identify key words in a text

What can you do well? ☑

What do you need to practice more? ☑

CHAPTER 7

SOCIOLOGY:
The Bystander Effect

SOCIOLOGY: the study of the development, structure, and functioning of human society

OBJECTIVES

To read academic texts, you need to master certain skills.

In this chapter, you will:

- Skim an introduction for main ideas

- Scan for specific facts

- Understand and use antonyms and synonyms

- Guess the meaning of words from the context

- Identify word forms from location in the sentence

- Understand collocations, or how words go together in English

- Use *wh-* questions to take notes

Consider These Questions

Look at the picture at the beginning of the chapter and discuss your opinion in a small group.

1. What is happening in the picture?
2. What reasons do you think people would give for not helping the man on the street?

READING ONE: Why and How Do We Help?

Ⓐ Warm-Up

Work with a partner and list the reasons why someone would help or not help a person in an emergency situation. Share your ideas with the class.

Why Someone Would Help	Why Someone Would Not Help
•	•
•	•
•	•

Ⓑ Reading Strategy

Skimming

Reading something quickly to find the main ideas or important facts is called **skimming**. To **skim**, read as fast as you can without stopping.

Skim the introduction to the reading. Then circle the correct word to complete the sentence below.

The more people that see an emergency happening, the **more/less** likely it is for the person in danger to receive help.

Now read the text to learn more.

Why and How Do We Help?

By Susan Krauss Whitbourne, Ph.D.
in *Psychology Today*

1   You've just **witnessed** an emergency in which someone in trouble needs help. Will you be the person to provide that help? According to the bystander effect, the larger the number of observers[1] of an emergency, the less likely it is that the **victim** will receive help. The bystander effect, first identified by researchers almost 50 years ago, holds that if you're the victim, you're better off if one person rather than a **crowd** is watching your distress.[2]

2   The theory of "diffusion of responsibility" is offered to explain the bystander effect. The theory states that people ask themselves: "Why should I help when there's someone else who could do it?"

3   In the hundreds of bystander studies, when the groups observing an emergency were friends, they were more likely to help than when group members were **strangers**. They were particularly likely to help when the person in need of help was also a friend or was someone they saw as similar to them in an important way.

4   The importance of "we-ness," feeling that another person is a member of your own group, is an

idea proposed by Yale psychologist John Dovidio and his colleagues, who have conducted extensive research on the factors that contribute to discrimination.

(continued on next page)

---

[1] *observers:* people who see or notice something

[2] *distress:* a feeling of extreme worry or sadness

5   Here are tips on how to **overcome** the pull of the bystander effect:

- If you're in trouble, pick out one person in the crowd. Making eye contact[3] with a stranger brings some "we-ness" into the situation.

- If you're a bystander, take action. Someone has to stand up[4] first when in a bystander situation. Let that person be you.

- Try not to worry about the **consequences** of helping. It's true that people who **intervene** in an emergency may be putting themselves at risk. But the **alternative** is to spend the rest of your life wondering if your actions might have saved someone else.

- **Model** altruism[5] and helping to the young. By showing that you have the guts[6] to help others in need, children will gain important lessons from you. It's up to us to decide whether to help our fellow humans when they're in need. We can be **passive** bystanders or we can step in and intervene. Within each of us is the capacity for heroism.

---

[3] *make eye contact:* look directly into another person's eyes while s/he is looking at you

[4] *stand up:* to support or defend someone or something when s/he or it is being attacked or criticized

[5] *altruism:* the practice of caring about needs of others before dealing with your own needs

[6] *guts:* the courage or determination you need to do something difficult or unpleasant

COMPREHENSION

A Main Ideas

Write the number of the paragraph in which you find each main idea from the reading.

1. Paragraph _____ defines "we-ness," which is feeling like you belong to a group.

2. Paragraph _____ defines the bystander effect.

3. Paragraph _____ explains practical ways to stop the bystander effect from happening.

4. Paragraph _____ explains why people in a group are less likely to help someone in an emergency situation.

5. Paragraph _____ describes the differences in the way people react to an emergency if they are part of a group of friends or a group of strangers.

Close Reading

Check (✓) the correct answer to each question.

1. Why are people less likely to help when they are with a group of people than when they are alone?

    ☐ **a.** They are scared.

    ☑ **b.** They think someone else will help.

    ☐ **c.** They think that the police will come and help.

2. When are we most likely to help people in an emergency situation?

    ☐ **a.** when we know the person

    ☐ **b.** when we don't know the person

    ☐ **c.** when the person needing help is a child

3. If you are in danger and there is a group of people around, what can you do to increase your chances of getting help?

    ☐ **a.** look at your cell phone

    ☐ **b.** look at one person in the crowd

    ☐ **c.** look at the people next to you and pretend they are your friends.

4. What advice does the author of this article give to bystanders?

    ☐ **a.** Only take risks if you are with some friends.

    ☐ **b.** Think carefully about helping before you do something.

    ☐ **c.** Be a leader and don't wait for others to do something first.

5. Why, according to the author, should you take action to help people in need?

    ☐ **a.** Taking action makes you a hero.

    ☐ **b.** Helping always has positive results.

    ☐ **c.** Doing something is better than worrying that you could have helped someone.

6. What is the final reason that witnesses need to take action?

    ☐ **a.** It's the law.

    ☐ **b.** We need to be brave.

    ☐ **c.** Children need role models.

VOCABULARY

A Antonyms

Two of the words in parentheses make sense in the sentence. Cross out the word that is the antonym (means the opposite) of the other two words. Compare your answers with a partner.

1. There was a large **crowd** (group/individual/mob) outside the movie theater when the victim was attacked.

2. It is not easy to **overcome** (defeat/beat/allow) fear.

3. If nobody **intervenes** (acts/helps/ hinders) in an emergency, the victim could die.

4. If you are the only witness to an emergency, you may feel that there is no other **alternative** (choice/option/necessity) besides helping.

5. Although he **witnessed** (ignored/perceived/saw) the emergency, he chose to do nothing.

B Guessing from Context

Find the words in bold in the reading and guess their meaning from the context. Then match each word with its meaning on the right.

__g__ 1. **witnessed**   a. people you do not know

____ 2. **victim**   b. someone who is in danger or is already hurt

____ 3. **strangers**   c. to behave in a way that provides a good example

____ 4. **consequences**

____ 5. **alternatives**   d. negative results

____ 6. **model**   e. inactive

____ 7. **passive**   f. options

                             g. observed

C Word Usage

Complete the paragraph with words from the box.

alternatives	crowd	intervene	stranger	victim	witnesses

According to the bystander effect, _____witnesses_____ are more

1.

likely to _____ when they are alone than when they are

2.

part of a _____. That is, a _____ has

3.   4.

a better chance of getting help from a _____ when the

5.

bystander thinks that there are no other _____.

6.

CRITICAL THINKING

Discuss the questions in a small group. Be prepared to share your opinions with the class.

1. Does the bystander effect surprise you? Explain why or why not.

2. Is this article based on opinion or fact? What details does the writer include in paragraphs 1, 3, and 4 that support your answer?

3. In paragraph 5, the author presents tips for overcoming the bystander effect. Which tip is the most effective, in your opinion? Why?

A Warm-Up

Discuss the questions in a small group.

1. Do you like reading about real people? Why or why not?

2. Do you think ordinary people can be heroes? Share some examples with your group.

B Reading Strategy

Scanning

Scanning is useful when looking for specific facts. To **scan**, quickly look over the text to find the necessary information.

Scan the reading and answer these questions for each situation.

CASE NUMBER	DID THIS HAPPEN IN THE MORNING, THE AFTERNOON, OR AT NIGHT?	WHO WAS IN DANGER?	DID THE BYSTANDERS INTERVENE?
1			
2			

Now read the case studies to learn more about bystanders.

Case Studies

Kitty's Story

1   In a **serene**, tree-lined, mostly residential neighborhood in the Kew Gardens section of Queens, New York, a **violent** murder took place on March 13, 1964. Kitty Genovese, a 28-year-old woman, parked her car close to her apartment as she always did after her night job ended. It was 3:20 A.M., and the residents of this middle-class area, which looked more like a small village in the suburbs than a city neighborhood, were fast asleep. Kitty was followed by an attacker and stabbed.[1] She screamed, "Oh my God! He stabbed me!"

_____
[1] *stabbed:* injured with a sharp object

2   Apartment lights went on as Kitty's neighbors were woken by her **shrieks**. Robert Mozer, who lived on the seventh floor, opened his window and shouted, "Hey, let that girl alone!" The **assailant** walked away, and Kitty, who was bleeding badly, tried to get up and reach her building. Five minutes later, Kitty was stabbed again and screamed, "I'm dying! I'm dying!" Lights went on in many apartments. At 3:50 A.M., Kitty's attacker came back and stabbed her **fatally** for the third time. Then, a neighbor called the police. When the police arrived two minutes later, the 70-year-old man who had called them and one other man were the only witnesses on the street. At 4:25 A.M., the ambulance arrived, and that is when the witnesses came out.

3   Catherine Genovese, known as Kitty, was the oldest of five siblings born to Italian immigrants. She was a hard-working young woman who dreamed of opening her own Italian restaurant. Martin Gansberg's *New York Times* article written on March 27, 1964, shocked the nation. Not only was a young woman brutally[2] murdered, but the 38 witnesses failed to call the police.

(continued on next page)

_____
[2] *brutally:* violently

Wesley's Bravery

4   At 12:45 P.M. early in January of 2007, passengers waited on the platform at 137th Street and Broadway in New York City. Wesley Autrey, a 50-year-old construction worker and Navy veteran, was standing with his four- and six-year-old daughters. Nearby, a man **collapsed**. Autrey and two women were able to help him stand up, but then something shocking happened. Cameron Hollopeter, 20, fell onto the tracks as the lights from the Number 1 train appeared. Within seconds, Autrey jumped on top of Hollopeter and pressed him down into the 12-inch-deep space between the two tracks. Five train cars passed over Autrey and Hollopeter before the train could stop. Power was turned off, and both Autrey and Hollopeter were **rescued**. Miraculously, neither man was seriously **injured**.

5   The next day Autrey went to visit Hollopeter and his family in the hospital. "Mr. Autrey's **instinctive** and **unselfish** act saved our son's life," Hollopeter's father said. "There are no words to properly express our gratitude[3] and feelings for his actions." However, Wesley Autrey told the *New York Times*, "I don't feel like I did something spectacular;[4] I just saw someone who needed help. I did what I felt was right."

_____

[3] *gratitude:* thankfulness

[4] *spectacular:* very impressive or exciting

COMPREHENSION

A Main Ideas

Read each statement. Decide if it is *True* or *False* according to the reading. Check (✓) the appropriate box. If it is false, change it to make it true.

	TRUE	FALSE
1. After Kitty Genovese was attacked the first time, her neighbors woke up.	☐	☐
2. Genovese was killed after she was stabbed the second time.	☐	☐
3. It took the police a long time to arrive.	☐	☐
4. Most of her neighbors were outside when the police arrived.	☐	☐
5. Genovese's parents owned an Italian restaurant.	☐	☐
6. Wesley Autrey was waiting for the subway with his wife.	☐	☐
7. Autrey waited a few minutes before deciding to help Hollopeter.	☐	☐
8. The train stopped seconds before it got to where Autrey and Hollopeter were.	☐	☐
9. Autrey was shocked by how he acted.	☐	☐

B Close Reading

Find these numbers in each case study. Write the noun each describes next to it.

Case 1:

28-year-old _____

seventh _____

five _____

two _____

70-year-old _____

38 _____

(continued on next page)

Case 2:

50-year-old _____

four- and six-year-old _____

1 _____

12-inch-deep _____

two _____

VOCABULARY

Ⓐ Parts of Speech

Look at the words in the box. Locate each word in the reading and look at how it is used in a sentence. Sort the words according to their parts of speech and list them in the chart. If you need more information, see page 6 for descriptions of the parts of speech.

| assailant | injured | rescued | shrieks | violent |
| collapsed | instinctive | serene | unselfish | |

Nouns	Verbs	Adjectives
shrieks		

Ⓑ Collocations

> When **words** are **used together regularly**, they become a pair and are called **collocations**. The word pairing is not for grammatical reasons, but because of the association with each other. For example, we say "fast food" but "a quick meal."

Find the words in the reading and write the word each is used with.

1. serene ___*neighborhood*___

2. violent _____

3. fatally _____

4. injured _____

5. unselfish _____

Synonyms

Work with a partner. Read the reading again and discuss the meanings of the words in bold. Then match each word with its synonym (word with the same meaning).

_h_	1. serene	**a.**	screams
____	2. shrieks	**b.**	brutal
____	3. assailant	**c.**	saved
____	4. fatally	**d.**	attacker
____	5. collapsed	**e.**	natural
____	6. rescued	**f.**	hurt
____	7. injured	**g.**	generous
____	8. instinctive	**h.**	peaceful
____	9. unselfish	**i.**	fell down
____	10. violent	**j.**	deadly

NOTE-TAKING: Using *Wh-* Questions

Go back to the reading and read it again. Each time you come across information that answers *who*, *what*, *where*, *when*, *why*, or *how*, underline that information. Then write the question word in the margin.

where
when
who

In a **serene**, tree-lined, mostly residential neighborhood in the Kew Gardens section of Queens, New York, a **violent** murder took place on March 13, 1964. Kitty Genovese, a 28-year-old woman, parked her car close to her apartment as she always did after her night job ended. It was 3:20 A.M., and the residents of this middle-class area, which looked more like a small village in the suburbs than a city neighborhood, were fast asleep. Kitty was followed by an attacker and stabbed.[1] She screamed, "Oh my God! He stabbed me!"

CRITICAL THINKING

Discuss the questions in a small group. Be prepared to share your opinions with the class.

1. Which case is a better example of the bystander effect in your opinion? Why?

2. Does the bystander effect hold true in your native country? Explain.

3. What do we know about Wesley Autrey that might have made him more likely to intervene than other bystanders?

4. Do you consider Autrey a hero? Why or why not?

AFTER YOU READ

WRITING ACTIVITY

Choose one of the topics and write an interview. Use at least five of the words and phrases you studied in the chapter (for a complete list, go to page 105).

1. Write an interview with a psychologist who is studying the bystander effect.

2. Write an interview between Wesley Autrey and a newspaper reporter.

DISCUSSION AND WRITING TOPICS

Discuss these topics in a small group. Choose one of them and write a paragraph or two about it. Use the vocabulary from the chapter.

1. Do you think the bystander effect is as likely to take place today considering all our advances in technology? Why or why not?

2. How could we as a society try to reduce the bystander effect? Think of specific examples and give detailed descriptions.

VOCABULARY

Nouns	Verbs	Adjectives	Adverb
alternative*	collapsed*	instinctive	fatally
assailant	injured*	passive*	
consequences*	intervene*	serene	
crowd	model	unselfish	
shrieks	overcome	violent	
strangers	rescued		
victim	witnessed		

* = AWL (Academic Word List) item

SELF-ASSESSMENT

In this chapter you learned to:

○ Skim an introduction for main ideas

○ Scan for specific facts

○ Understand and use antonyms and synonyms

○ Guess the meaning of words from the context

○ Identify word forms from location in the sentence

○ Understand collocations, or how words go together in English

○ Use *wh-* questions to take notes

What can you do well? ☑

What do you need to practice more? ☑

CHAPTER 8

GOVERNMENT:
Interpreting the Law

GOVERNMENT: the group of people who make laws and determine how a country will be run

OBJECTIVES

To read academic texts, you need to master certain skills.

In this chapter, you will:

- Identify key words and phrases in topic sentences to understand main ideas

- Predict the content of a text after identifying the text type

- Understand and use synonyms

- Guess the meaning of words from the context

- Determine whether a word has a positive or negative meaning

- Use a dictionary to learn different meanings of words and word forms

- Complete a timeline

The Capitol

The White House

The Supreme Court Building

Consider This Diagram

Look at the diagram of how the United States government is organized under the Constitution. Answer these questions with a partner.

1. What are the names of the three branches (parts) of the U.S. government?

2. Why do you think there are three branches of the U.S. government?

3. Which branch of the U.S. government makes final decisions about the law?

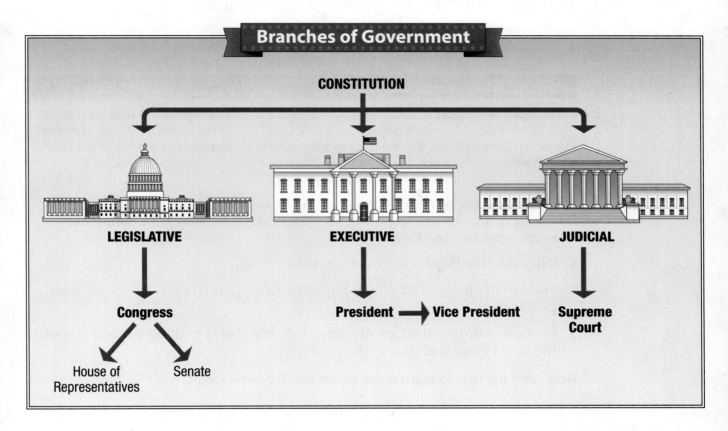

A Warm-Up

Check (✓) all the statements you think are true. Share your answers with a partner. Try to give a reason why you think the statement is true or false.

☐ **1.** The justice who served the longest on the Supreme Court served for a little more than 36 years.

☐ **2.** George Washington appointed[1] the most Supreme Court justices.

☐ **3.** Three presidents were also Supreme Court justices.

B Reading Strategy

Identifying Key Words and Phrases

The **topic sentence** is usually the first sentence of a paragraph. It tells the reader the main idea of the paragraph. You do not have to understand every word in the topic sentence to get the main idea. **Key words or phrases** in the topic sentence can help you figure out the main idea.

Underline the key words or phrases in the topic sentence of each paragraph in the reading. Try not to circle more than three words in each topic sentence. Then answer the questions.

1. Why was the Supreme Court created?

2. How many justices sit on the Supreme Court, and how do they get their positions?

3. Is understanding the Constitution (U.S. laws) and making decisions about the law a clear and simple process?

Now read the text to learn more about the Supreme Court.

---

[1] *appointed:* chosen for a job or position

Our Supreme Court—An Introduction

**By Nadine Strossen
from the introduction to
Our Supreme Court
By Richard Panchyk**

1   The Supreme Court was created to protect and interpret[1] the Constitution and laws of the United States. It exists to protect the freedom of all Americans. The U.S. Supreme Court is often at the center of public attention since it has so much power as the interpreter of the U.S. Constitution. This means that the Supreme Court justices can overturn[2] decisions by **elected** officials, including the president and Congress.[3]

2   The court's nine justices are not **elected**, but are appointed by the president, with the Senate's[4] agreement. Like other federal[5] judges, they have their jobs for life. Supreme Court justices do not have to explain their actions to the people of the United States, unlike elected officials. Their **independence** makes it easier for the justices to **enforce** the Constitution **neutrally**, even when they need to support individuals and groups who **lack** political power, or are unpopular. However, the Supreme Court is at times criticized when it allows rights not specifically **mentioned** in the Constitution.

3   The **debates** about the meaning of the Constitution, and the power of the Supreme Court to interpret it, go back to the **founding** of the United States. These debates will never end, since they reflect questions about how to strike a balance[6] between the government's power and individual freedom. Therefore, no matter what the court decides, it will always be criticized by some people. Nonetheless, public opinion **surveys** show that, in general, the Supreme Court is one of the most highly respected and trusted organizations in the whole country. The court is also widely respected around the world and has served as a **model** for courts in many other democracies[7] that protect human rights. The mission of the court is **summarized** by the words written on the Supreme Court's building in Washington, D.C.: "Equal Justice under the Law."

---

[1] *interpret:* to explain or decide on the meaning of an event or statement

[2] *overturn:* to change a decision made by a court so that it is the opposite of what it was before

[3] *Congress:* the group of people elected to make laws for the United States, consisting of the Senate and the House of Representatives

[4] *Senate:* the smaller of the two groups that make laws in the United States

[5] *federal:* relating to the central government of a country that consists of several states

[6] *strike a balance:* to give the correct amount of attention or importance to two opposing ideas or situations

[7] *democracies:* systems of government in which citizens in a country can vote to elect leaders

COMPREHENSION

Ⓐ Main Ideas

Circle the word or phrase that correctly completes each sentence.

1. The Supreme Court protects the **freedom/power** of all Americans.

2. The Supreme Court **can/cannot** change a decision made by the legislative and executive branches of government.

3. Supreme Court justices **can/cannot** serve on the highest court in the United States for as long as they want to.

4. The power of Supreme Court justices is **similar to/different from** that of elected officials.

5. Public opinion about the power of the Supreme Court **has changed/ has not changed** recently.

Ⓑ Close Reading

Complete each sentence on the left with a phrase on the right.

_c_ 1. The Supreme Court has the power to change	a. answer to the public about their decisions.
___ 2. Supreme Court justices do not have to	b. respected organization in the United States and in democracies around the world.
___ 3. Supreme Court justices are responsible for	c. decisions made by the president and Congress.
___ 4. Because it is not easy to find a balance between people's freedom and the government's power,	d. the Supreme Court is often criticized.
___ 5. The Supreme Court is a widely	e. fairly protecting the rights of all Americans.

VOCABULARY

A Synonyms

Cross out the word in parentheses that is NOT a synonym for (word with the same meaning as) the word in bold. Compare answers with a partner.

1. The president of the United States is **elected** (chosen, appointed, selected) every four years.

2. Because the Supreme Court judges are not elected to their positions, they have **independence** (freedom, liberty, dependence) from the public and can make decisions fairly based on the law.

3. When you make a decision **neutrally** (impartially, subjectively, objectively), you try to be as fair as possible.

4. The **founding** (beginning, ending, start) of the United States goes back to 1776.

B Definitions

Find each word on the left in the reading and match it with its definition.

_e_ 1. **enforce**   a. not have something or not have enough of it

___ 2. **lack**   b. gave only the main information

___ 3. **mentioned**   c. discussions or arguments on a subject in which people express different opinions

___ 4. **debates**

___ 5. **surveys**   d. said or written about in a few words

___ 6. **summarized**   e. make people obey a rule or law

f. questions that ask a large number of people about their opinion or behavior

C Word Forms

Fill in the chart with the correct word forms. Use a dictionary if necessary. An **X** indicates there is no form in that category.

	NOUN	VERB	ADJECTIVE
1.			neutral
2.		X	independent
3.		elect	
4.		summarize	X
5.		lack	X
6.	survey		X

CRITICAL THINKING

Discuss the questions with a partner. Be prepared to share your ideas with the class.

1. What might be some advantages and disadvantages to a Supreme Court justice serving for life?

2. Under what circumstances should a Supreme Court justice be impeached, or "fired"?

3. What factors might cause Supreme Court justices to have different interpretations of the Constitution?

READING TWO: Supreme Court Justice Sonia Sotomayor

A Warm-Up

Work with a partner. Describe a person who has inspired you. Explain how and why he or she inspired you. Give as many details as possible.

B Reading Strategy

Identifying Type of Text

Identifying the **type of text** you are about to read will help you determine what kind of information you can expect to find in that text.

The reading is a biography, or story of someone's life. Check (✓) the information that you expect to find in this biography about Sonia Sotomayor.

☐ date of birth

☐ place of birth

☐ parents' background

☐ siblings

☐ social class

☐ education

☐ hobbies

☐ marital status

☐ career

Now read the text to learn about the life of Justice Sotomayor.

Supreme Court Justice Sonia Sotomayor

had spoken mostly Spanish before their father's death. Sonia Sotomayor became an **avid** reader and **aspired** to become like the detective Nancy Drew in the children's mystery series she loved to read.

1 For many, graduating at the top of their class would be the highlight of their life. But for Sonia Sotomayor, her early **accomplishments** were just the beginning. In 2009, Sonia Sotomayor became the first Hispanic Supreme Court justice and the third woman to serve on the highest court in the United States. While this accomplishment is remarkable and **rare**—only 112 people have served as U.S. Supreme Court justices—her journey from a public housing project[1] in the South Bronx to the Supreme Court is equally inspirational. President Obama rightly described Sotomayor as a symbol of the American dream.

2 Born in 1954 to parents who had moved from Puerto Rico to New York during World War II, Sotomayor did not have an easy start in life. Her father died when she was nine years old, and her mother, a nurse, **brought up** Sotomayor and her brother alone. Celine Sotomayor **emphasized** to her children the importance of education. She insisted that her children become fluent in English even though they

3 Sotomayor's mother worked six days a week to make ends meet.[2] She showed by example the value of hard work. As a result, Sotomayor learned to work hard, and she overcame **obstacles** such as managing her juvenile diabetes.[3] After Sotomayor graduated high school as valedictorian[4] and received a scholarship to Princeton University, she went to Yale Law School, where she continued to **excel** academically. One of her former Yale classmates, Robert Klonoff, remembers her intellectual toughness from law school: "She would stand up for herself[5] and not be **intimidated** by anyone."[6]

(continued on next page)

---

[1] **public housing project:** apartments supported by the government for low-income individuals

[2] **make ends meet:** to make enough money to pay the bills

[3] **juvenile diabetes:** a disease in which young people have too much sugar in their blood

[4] **valedictorian:** the student who graduates with the highest grades from his or her high school class

[5] **stand up for herself:** defend her opinions

[6] *Washington Post,* 5/7/09

4   Before becoming a Supreme Court justice, Sotomayor worked at almost every level of the judicial system. After graduating from Yale, Sotomayor became an assistant district attorney (DA) in Manhattan in 1979. For more than five years, Sotomayor prosecuted[6] dozens of criminal cases. In 1992, she began her judicial career and tried[7] approximately 450 cases as a U.S. district judge for the Southern District of New York. During this time, she ended the major league baseball strike,[8] which had been the longest in the history of professional sports.

_____

[6] *prosecuted:* took legal action against someone in a court of law

[7] *tried:* conducted a legal case in court

[8] In 1994 – 95, professional baseball was not played for 232 days due to a disagreement between players and team owners, considered the worst work stoppage in sports history.

5   Sotomayor is known to be **sharp**, outspoken, and fearless and has been successful as both a professional and a community leader. She has motivated other judges to bring young women to the courthouse on Take Your Daughter to Work Day. She is also responsible for creating the Development School for Youth program, which has 16 weekly workshops to teach inner-city high school students about how to function in the workplace. Each semester about 70 students participate in this program led by Sotomayor and corporate executives. Like her mother, Sonia Sotomayor continues to teach by example.

COMPREHENSION

A Main Ideas

Check (✓) each possible answer.

According to this biography, Sonia Sotomayor . . .

☐ **1.** is very intelligent.

☐ **2.** grew up in an upper-class neighborhood.

☐ **3.** is bilingual (speaks two languages fluently).

☐ **4.** is a very hard worker.

☐ **5.** knows how to deal with challenges.

☐ **6.** got a scholarship to Princeton University.

☐ **7.** went to Yale Law School.

☐ **8.** is very confident in her opinions and beliefs.

☐ **9.** has had many different kinds of experience in her career.

☐ **10.** spends time helping youth.

B Close Reading

Match the numbers on the left with the descriptions on the right.

_e_ **1.** 1st   **a.** cases tried as a district judge

____ **2.** 3rd   **b.** days a week her mother worked

____ **3.** 9   **c.** female Supreme Court justice

____ **4.** 6   **d.** inner-city students in program each semester

____ **5.** 5   **e.** Hispanic Supreme Court justice

____ **6.** 450   **f.** age when her father died

____ **7.** 16   **g.** years as an assistant DA

____ **8.** 70   **h.** weekly workshops for inner-city youth

VOCABULARY

A Using the Dictionary

For some words, there is more than one meaning in the dictionary. You must choose the correct meaning in the context.

> **rare** *adjective* **1** meat that has only been cooked for a short time and is red **2** not seen or found very often, or not happening very often
>
> **obstacle** *noun* **1** something that makes it difficult for you to succeed **2** something that blocks your way, so that you must go around it
>
> **sharp** *adjective* **1** able to cut something; having a very thin edge or point that can easily cut things **2** stylish; fashionable **3** clever; quick-witted

Write the number of the definition that is used for each word in the reading.

____ **1.** "While this accomplishment is remarkable and **rare** — only 112 people have served as U.S. Supreme Court justices — her journey from a public house project in the South Bronx to the Supreme Court is equally inspirational." (*paragraph 1*)

____ **2.** "As a result, Sotomayor learned to work hard, and she overcame **obstacles** such as managing her juvenile diabetes." (*paragraph 3*)

____ **3.** "Sotomayor is known to be **sharp**, outspoken, and fearless, and has been successful as both a professional and a community leader." (*paragraph 5*)

B Guessing from Context

1 Look at the list of words from the reading. Locate each word in the reading and try to guess its meaning from the context clues. Write down the clue(s) that help you guess the meaning.

1. accomplishments   _graduating at the top of their class_

2. brought up   _____

3. rare   _____

4. emphasized   _____

5. avid   _____

6. aspired   _____

7. obstacles   _____

8. excel   _____

9. intimidated   _____

10. sharp   _____

2 Match each word with its definition or synonym.

_g_ 1. **accomplishments**   a. raised

___ 2. **brought up**   b. enthusiastic; passionate

___ 3. **emphasized**   c. do extremely well

___ 4. **avid**   d. pointed out the importance
                                      of something

___ 5. **aspired**
                                   e. frightened

___ 6. **excel**
                                   f. hoped; aimed

___ 7. **intimidated**
                                   g. successes

C Connotations

> Some words have **feelings** connected to them depending on how they are used in a sentence. These feelings, or **connotations,** can be **positive** (good or useful) or **negative** (bad or harmful).

Look at each word. Find the word in the reading. Decide whether it has a *Positive* or *Negative* meaning. Check the appropriate box. Discuss your answers with a partner.

	POSITIVE	NEGATIVE
1. accomplishments	☐	☐
2. rare	☐	☐
3. avid	☐	☐
4. aspired	☐	☐
5. obstacles	☐	☐
6. excel	☐	☐
7. intimidated	☐	☐
8. sharp	☐	☐

NOTE-TAKING: Complete a Timeline

A timeline can help you keep the events in a reading in order. It is especially useful when reading about a person. Write the important events in Sonia Sotomayor's life next to the appropriate date in the timeline.

1954
1963
1972
1976
1979
1992
2009

CRITICAL THINKING

Discuss the questions with a partner. Be prepared to share your ideas with the class.

1. President Obama said that Sonia Sotomayor's journey symbolizes the American dream. What do you think this means?

2. What qualities and qualifications does Sotomayor have that make her a valuable Supreme Court justice?

3. If you could meet Sotomayor, what questions would you want to ask her?

4. Do you find Sonia Sotomayor's life story inspiring? Why or Why not?"

AFTER YOU READ

WRITING ACTIVITY

Choose one of the topics. Use at least five of the words and phrases you studied in the chapter (for a complete list, go to page 119).

1. If you were a member of Congress and were interviewing a potential Supreme Court justice, what questions would you ask? What would you want to know before you confirmed a candidate? Write three questions.

2. Read about the current Supreme Court justices. Write a paragraph about one of the justices you find interesting.

DISCUSSION AND WRITING TOPICS

Discuss these topics in a small group. Choose one of them and write a paragraph about it. Use the vocabulary from the chapter.

1. Should all judges be in their jobs for life? Why do you think some judges are elected and some are appointed?

2. Do you think it is a difficult job to be a Supreme Court justice? Why or why not?

VOCABULARY

Nouns	Verbs	Adjectives	Adverb
accomplishments	aspire	avid	neutrally*
debates*	bring up	elected	
founding*	emphasize*	rare	
independence	enforce*	sharp	
obstacles	excel		
surveys*	intimidate		
	lack		
	mention		
	summarize*		

* = AWL (Academic Word List) item

SELF-ASSESSMENT

In this chapter you learned to:

○ Identify key words and phrases in topic sentences to understand main ideas

○ Predict the content of a text after identifying the text type

○ Understand and use synonyms

○ Guess the meaning of words from the context

○ Determine whether a word has a positive or negative meaning

○ Use a dictionary to learn different meanings of words and word forms

○ Complete a timeline

What can you do well? ☑

What do you need to practice more? ☑

CHAPTER 9

ECONOMICS: Bartering in the 21st Century

ECONOMICS: the study of the way in which money, goods, and services are produced and used

OBJECTIVES

To read academic texts, you need to master certain skills.

In this chapter, you will:

- Predict the content of a text from the title

- Preview a text using visuals

- Understand and use antonyms and synonyms

- Determine whether a word has a positive or negative meaning

- Guess the meaning of words from the context

- Use a dictionary to find word forms

- Understand and use prepositions

- Use underlining to identify important facts in a text

Consider This Definition

> **Collaborative consumption** is the cultural and economic model in which sharing, swapping, bartering, trading, or renting have become easy due to advances in social media and peer-to-peer online platforms.

Discuss the questions in a small group.

1. What are some items that you have at home that you don't use but cannot throw away in the garbage?

2. Would you be willing to trade these things for other items you want? Why or why not?

3. How might advances in technology make collaborative consumption popular?

Bartering and trading are a way of life in some cultures.

READING ONE: Swap Tree—Simple, Easy Online Trading

A Warm-Up

Check (✓) the items that you would NOT be willing to trade online. Discuss with a partner why you would not be comfortable trading the items you checked.

- ☐ **1.** books
- ☐ **2.** music
- ☐ **3.** movies
- ☐ **4.** skills (talents, expertise)
- ☐ **5.** your car for a short period of time
- ☐ **6.** your apartment or house while you are away
- ☐ **7.** money

Predicting Content from the Title

Predicting is a very important pre-reading skill. When you **predict**, you make a guess about something based on the information you have. Predicting helps prepare the reader for the reading experience that is to come. The title of a text can often help you predict what the text might be about.

Read the title of the reading. With a partner check (✓) the ideas you think might be true about the reading.

☐ **1.** Swap Tree is the name of a company.

☐ **2.** People can exchange items if they go to this website.

☐ **3.** The website is not difficult for people to use.

Now read the text to see if your predictions are correct.

Swap Tree—Simple, Easy Online Trading

By Josh Smith in DailyFinance.com

1　If you're anything like the average **consumer** you have shelves full of used media: books, games, movies, and music. Unfortunately, the amount of money received from selling on eBay and other sites is almost not **worth the time** and money you spend listing,[1] packaging, and shipping. But if you trade items using SwapTree.com you might be able to turn your trashy[2] romance novel into a copy of *Treasure Island*.

---

[1] *listing:* entering information about something

[2] *trashy:* of extremely bad quality

2 Swap Tree launched[3] in 2007 and has grown quite a bit, adding new **features** and more users to make **swapping** your old books, movies, games, and music easier than ever. The site has a large catalog of items to trade for, most likely because all the other users have as much stuff as you do!

3 When I listed *Gears of War 2*, an old yet enjoyable video game, for trade, I was presented with more than 9,000 trade **opportunities** for everything from personal finance books to Wii games and a surplus[4] of items in between. I could then choose who I wanted to trade with based on the item's condition, location, and trader rating.[5]

4 Swap Tree is free to use. The only thing you have to pay for is shipping, which is pretty cheap, since you can ship most items using Media Mail service from the USPS.[6] To make it even easier, you can print postage at home, based on your item's weight in the Swap Tree database, and drop it in your local mailbox. If you'd rather not **deal with** mailing anything at all use the location search to find trades in your city.

5 One of the few **drawbacks** to the service is its **simplicity**. As WalletPop pointed out last year you can't combine items for trade, so you won't be able to offer three **mediocre** movies for a new release. All trades are one for one. Even with this drawback Swap Tree is a great way to get the best value for your used games, movies, books, and music without a **hassle**, and the Swap Tree Tools make it easier to use than many other barter sites.[7]

---

[3] *launched:* started

[4] *surplus:* more of something than is needed or used

[5] *trader rating:* the opinion about the person trading the item

[6] *Media Mail service from the USPS:* an inexpensive way to ship media using the U.S. Postal Service

[7] *barter sites:* trading websites

COMPREHENSION

Ⓐ **Main Ideas**

Read each statement. Decide if it is *True* or *False* according to the reading. Check (✓) the appropriate box. If it is false, change it to make it true. Discuss your answers with a partner.

	TRUE	FALSE
1. We all have a lot of media we don't use anymore.	☐	☐
2. Swap Tree has a long list of items to trade.	☐	☐
3. You can only trade the same type of items.	☐	☐
4. You can only trade via mail.	☐	☐
5. You can trade three old books for one new book.	☐	☐

Close Reading

Answer the questions. Then discuss your answers with a partner.

1. Why don't people make more money when they sell things on sites like eBay?

2. What three factors can people use to help them when making a trade?

3. What example does the author give in paragraph 4 to show the reader that trading on Swap Tree is easy?

4. What reason does the author give in paragraph 5 for using Swap Tree?

VOCABULARY

A **Antonyms**

Find each word in the left column in the reading. Use the context to determine its meaning. Then choose the word on the right that is its antonym (word with the opposite meaning).

_b_ 1. consumer   a. pleasure

___ 2. drawbacks   b. seller

___ 3. simplicity   c. excellent

___ 4. mediocre   d. difficulty

___ 5. hassle   e. advantages

B **Connotations**

> Some words have **feelings** connected to them depending on how they are used in a sentence. These feelings, or **connotations**, can be **positive** (good or useful) or **negative** (bad or harmful).

Look at each word or phrase. Find it in the reading. Decide whether it has a *Positive* or *Negative* meaning. Check (✓) the appropriate box. Discuss your answers with a partner.

	POSITIVE	NEGATIVE
1. worth the time	☐	☐
2. opportunities	☐	☐
3. drawbacks	☐	☐
4. mediocre	☐	☐
5. hassle	☐	☐

C Synonyms

Complete each sentence with a word or phrase from the box. Use the synonym (word or phrase with the same meaning) in parentheses to help you select the correct word or phrase. Compare answers with a partner.

deal with	features	swapping	worth the time

1. Selling used items online might not be _____ if the
   (beneficial)
   seller's costs are too high.

2. One of Swap Tree's key _____ is that you can find out
   (characteristics)
   the quality of items.

3. _____ is a great way to get new things and get rid of
   (trading)
   old items that you don't want anymore.

4. If you prefer not to _____ the post office, you can also
   (work with)
   trade items face-to-face by using Swap Tree.

NOTE-TAKING: Underlining Key Facts

Go back to the reading and read it again. Underline two important facts in each paragraph that would help you explain what Swap Tree is. Discuss your answers with a partner.

CRITICAL THINKING

Discuss the questions with a partner. Be prepared to share your answers with the class.

1. In paragraph 1, the author mentions the book *Treasure Island*. Do you think this is considered high-quality literature? Give a reason from the paragraph to support your answer.

2. What adjectives does Swap Tree use to describe its website? Do you think these are good selling points? Why or why not?

3. Swap Tree also makes it possible for people to trade face-to-face. Do you think this is a good idea? Would you meet a stranger face-to-face from this website? Why or why not?

A Warm-Up

Discuss the meaning of this quote by Mahatma Gandhi with a small group.

"You must be the change you want to see in the world."

—*Mahatma Gandhi,* *the father of non-violent protests*

B Reading Strategy

Predicting Content from Visuals

Predicting is a very important pre-reading skill. When you **predict**, you make a guess about something based on the information you have. Predicting helps prepare the reader for the reading experience that is to come. Pictures in a text can often help you predict what the text is about.

Look at the photograph of Heidemarie Schwermer and check (✓) each idea you think could be true about her.

Heidemarie Schwermer . . .

☐ **1.** is a mother

☐ **2.** is a grandmother

☐ **3.** is in a movie

☐ **4.** doesn't like to spend money

Now read the text to see if your predictions are correct.

Heidemarie Schwermer

1   Can you imagine anyone choosing to live without money in our consumer society? Well, that's exactly what Heidemarie Schwermer has been doing since 1996 when she quit her job as a psychotherapist[1] and gave away all her **possessions**. This 69-year-old mother of two and grandmother of three has chosen to live a simple life without the pressure to buy and own. Schwermer has thought about

[1] *psychotherapist:* a professional who treats people with mental illness by discussing their problems rather than using medicine

possession and value since she was a young girl. Her family had to leave all their possessions in 1942 during World War II to **flee** from the Russian forces in Memel (former East Prussia). They couldn't take anything with them, and this made a great **impression** on her. Schwermer knew what it was like to be penniless and throughout her life has been troubled by poverty in the world. She knows from experience that possessions are not what give a person value.

2   Schwermer moved to Dortmund, a major city in Germany, with her two children in the late 1980s. She was so **shocked** by the homelessness² there that she decided to open a swap shop called Gib und Nimm (Give and Take) in 1994. Members of this group swap things and skills without money ever changing hands. What amazed Schwermer was not only how people's needs could be met, but also how much the participants **benefited** from the social **aspect** of their contact. At the swap shop, there is the potential for people to get to know one another and **bond**. This experience so deeply **moved**

² *homelessness:* state of living on the streets without a home

Schwermer that she decided to quit her job and not buy anything else without giving something away. Eventually, she was rid of all her material possessions, including her apartment. In 1996, Schwermer agreed to participate in a 12-month experiment that was made into a documentary film called *Living without Money*. However, at the end of the 12 months, she decided that living without money gave her "quality of life, inner wealth, and freedom."³ As a result, Schwermer continues to live without money.

3   Schwermer leads a nomadic⁴ life by trading practical skills such as gardening and cleaning, as well as her professional skills as a former teacher of 20 years and therapist, for food and a place to live for a short period of time. All her possessions fit into one suitcase and one backpack. In addition to making the documentary, she's written three books. She gives her **profits** away, however, and insists that her royalties⁵ be **donated** to charity.⁶ Schwermer lives a life based on the principle that we should not take more than we need. As Schwermer says, "I now feel that my own life is fantastic. I am a happy person who feels a membership to human beings and a big love for all of them."

³ http://shine.yahoo.com/work-money/ german-grandmother-lives-money-free- never-happier-173900934.html

⁴ *nomadic:* traveling from place to place without a permanent home

⁵ *royalties:* payments made to the writer of a book or piece of music, depending on sales

⁶ *charity:* an organization that gives money, goods, or help to people who need it

COMPREHENSION

A **Main Ideas**

Read the list of important events in Schwermer's life. Create a chronology by listing the events in the correct order on a separate sheet of paper. Go back to the reading and add the dates of the events on the left side of the chronology.

- As a young child during World War II, she had to leave her home with her family and couldn't take anything with her.
- She decided to continue living without money.
- She agreed to participate in a 12-month experiment that became a film called *Living without Money*.
- She moved to Dortmund, Germany, with her two children.
- She opened a swap shop called Gib und Nimm.
- She quit her job and promised not to buy anything new without giving something she owned away.

B **Close Reading**

Read each statement. Decide if it is *True* or *False* according to the reading. Check (✓) the appropriate box. If it is false, change it to make it true. Discuss your answers with a partner.

	TRUE	FALSE
1. Schwermer believes that there is a lot of stress in our society because of the pressure to buy and sell.	☐	☐
2. At the swap shop Gib und Nimm, participants trade only personal items.	☐	☐
3 Friendships have formed at Gib und Nimm.	☐	☐
4. Schwermer has an apartment.	☐	☐
5. Schwermer stays in one place for a long time.	☐	☐
6. Everything Schwermer owns fits into two bags.	☐	☐
7. Schwermer puts the money she makes from her books in the bank.	☐	☐

VOCABULARY

A Definitions

Find each word in the reading and match it with its definition.

__j__ 1. possessions	a. one part of a situation, plan, or subject
____ 2. flee	b. helped
____ 3. impression	c. the opinion or feeling you have about someone or something because of the way she, he, or it seems
____ 4. shocked	
____ 5. benefited	d. money that you gain by selling things or doing business
____ 6. aspect	e. to develop a special relationship with someone
____ 7. bond	f. to leave somewhere very quickly in order to escape from danger
____ 8. moved	g. surprised and usually upset or offended
____ 9. profits	h. given to a person or organization that needs help
____ 10. donated	i. made to feel strong emotion
	j. things that you own; belongings

B Word Forms

Fill in the chart with the correct word forms. Use a dictionary if necessary. An *X* indicates there is no form in that category.

	NOUN	VERB	ADJECTIVE
1.			shocked / shocking
2.	benefit		
3.	profit		
4.		donate	X
5.	impression		

C Prepositions

Complete each sentence with a preposition from the box. Then find the words in bold in the reading and check your answers. Some words will be used more than one time.

by	from	to

1. During times of war, many people have to **flee** _____*from*_____ their homeland.

2. The tourists were **shocked** _____ the poverty in the city.

3. We often **benefit** _____ challenging situations.

4. I was **moved** _____ the documentary *Living without Money*.

5. Have you ever **donated** your time or money _____ a charity?

CRITICAL THINKING

Discuss the questions with a partner. Be prepared to share your answers with the class.

1. What shocks you the most about Schwermer?

2. Do you think a child who grows up in a home where money is not spent has a different way of looking at the world than a child who grows up in a traditional Western household?

3. Is Heidemarie Schwermer a living example of Gandhi's words "You must be the change you want to see in the world." Give specific examples from the reading to support your answer.

4. What is your definition of inner wealth?

WRITING ACTIVITY

Make a list of what you buy in a day or a week. Then write a paragraph answering the questions. Use at least five of the words and phrases you studied in the chapter (for a complete list, go to page 132).

- Is everything you buy a necessity?
- Are there items you could choose not to buy, and it would not affect your life?
- Which items would be easiest to give up?

DISCUSSION AND WRITING TOPICS

Discuss these topics in a small group. Choose one of them and write a paragraph or two about it. Use the vocabulary from the chapter.

1. Would you have agreed to be part of an experiment to live without money? Why or why not?

2. What do you think you would miss the most if you lived without money for a time?

Could you choose to not buy food and eat what grows naturally around you?

VOCABULARY

Nouns	Verbs	Adjectives	Phrases and Idioms
aspect*	benefit*	mediocre	deal with
consumer*	bond	shocked	worth the time
drawbacks	donate		
features*	flee		
hassle	move		
impression	swap		
opportunities			
possessions			
profits			
simplicity			

* = AWL (Academic Word List) item

SELF-ASSESSMENT

In this chapter you learned to:

- ⭘ Predict the content of a text from the title
- ⭘ Preview a text using visuals
- ⭘ Understand and use antonyms and synonyms
- ⭘ Determine whether a word has a positive or negative meaning
- ⭘ Guess the meaning of words from the context
- ⭘ Use a dictionary to find word forms
- ⭘ Understand and use prepositions
- ⭘ Use underlining to identify important facts in a text

What can you do well? ☑

What do you need to practice more? ☑

CHAPTER 10

NEUROLOGY:
The Brain

NEUROLOGY: the study of the structure and function of nerves and the nervous system

OBJECTIVES

To read academic texts, you need to master certain skills.

In this chapter, you will:

- Scan a text to answer a question in the title

- Predict the type of text from the title

- Understand and use the prefix *un-*

- Determine whether a word has a positive or negative meaning

- Identify parts of speech

- Understand and use synonyms and antonyms

- Use dictionary entries to learn different meanings of a phrasal verb

- Categorize notes

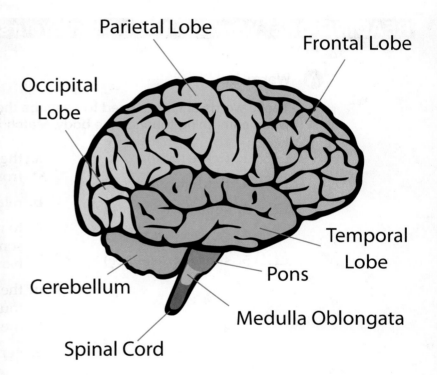

Parietal Lobe

Frontal Lobe

Occipital Lobe

Temporal Lobe

Pons

Cerebellum

Medulla Oblongata

Spinal Cord

Consider These Statements

Check (✓) all the statements you think are true. Share your answer with a partner.

☐ **1.** A baby's brain grows three times its size in the first year.

☐ **2.** Your brain stops growing when you are 18 years old.

☐ **3.** The left side of your brain controls the right side of your body, and the right side of your brain controls the left side of your body.

☐ **4.** Your brain is 75% water.

☐ **5.** Your brain is very sensitive to pain.

READING ONE: Why Can't You Tickle Yourself?

Ⓐ Warm-Up

These words are often used to describe the way the brain transmits information when something touches the body. Match the words with their definitions.

_____ **1. tickle** (*verb*)

_____ **2. ticklish** (*adjective*)

_____ **3. sensation** (*noun*)

_____ **4. senses** (*noun*)

_____ **5. sensory** (*adjective*)

a. the ability to feel, or a feeling you get from one of your five senses

b. relating to your senses

c. to move your fingers lightly over someone's body in order to make him/her laugh

d. the five natural ways (sight, hearing, touch, taste, and smell) of experiencing the world

e. very easy to tickle

Ⓑ Reading Strategy

Scanning to Answer a Question in the Title

Scanning is useful when looking for specific facts. To **scan**, quickly look over the text to find the necessary information. For example, you can scan a text to find the answer to a question in the title.

The title of the reading is a question. Scan the first paragraph of the text to find the sentence that answers this question. Underline the sentence.

Now read the text to find out more.

WHY CAN'T YOU TICKLE YOURSELF?

from *Welcome to Your Brain* By Sandra Aamodt and Sam Wang

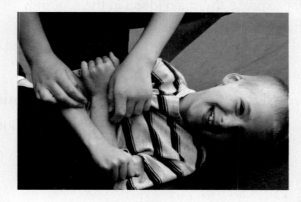

1   When doctors examine a ticklish patient, they place the patient's hands over theirs during the exam to prevent the tickling sensation. Why does this work? Because no matter how ticklish you may be, you can't tickle yourself. Go ahead. Try it. The reason is that with every move you make, part of your brain is busy predicting the sensory **consequences** of that movement. For instance, as we write, we are **unaware** of the feel of the chair and the texture[1] of our socks. Yet we'd immediately notice a tap[2] on the shoulder. If the only information your brain received was **pure** touch sensation, you wouldn't be able to tell whether someone was punching[3] your shoulder or whether you'd just bumped into[4] a wall. Since you'd want to react very differently to those two situations, it's important for your brain to be able to **tell them apart**.

2   How does your brain **accomplish** this goal? To study this, scientists in London developed, of all things, a tickling machine. When a person presses a button, a robot arm brushes[5] a piece of foam across the person's own hand. If the robot arm brushes the hand as soon as the person presses the button, the person feels the sensation, but it doesn't tickle. However, a delay of one-fifth of a second is enough to **fool** the brain into thinking the robot's touch has been delivered by someone else—and then it tickles.

3   This means that some brain **region** must be able to **distinguish** your own touch from someone else's. The experimenters found one: the cerebellum, whose name means "little brain." The cerebellum is in an ideal location for distinguishing expected from **unexpected** sensations. It receives sensory information of nearly every type. In addition, it receives a copy of all the movement commands sent out by the motor centers[6] of the brain. For this reason, researchers suggest that the cerebellum uses the movement commands to make a prediction of the consequences of each movement. If this prediction matches the actual sensory information, then the brain knows it's safe to **ignore** the sensation because it's not important. If reality does not match the prediction, then something surprising has happened— and you might need to pay attention.

[1] *texture:* the way a surface or material feels when you touch it, and how smooth or rough it looks

[2] *tap:* an act of hitting something gently, especially in order to get someone's attention

[3] *punching:* hitting someone or something hard with your fist (closed hand)

[4] *bumped into:* hit or knocked against something, especially by accident

[5] *brushes:* lightly touches with an object

[6] *motor centers:* the area in the brain that controls muscles

COMPREHENSION

A **Main Ideas**

Check (✓) the statements that best express the main ideas in the reading.
Discuss your answers with a partner.

☐ 1. Doctors can help patients feel more comfortable during an exam.

☐ 2. Our brains predicts the result of every move we make.

☐ 3. The way the scientists invented the "tickling machine" was fascinating.

☐ 4. Our brains help us decide how to react to different physical sensations.

B **Close Reading**

Circle the correct answer.

1. If you put your hand on top of the hand of someone who is touching you, the brain sends a message that you **are/are not** touching yourself.

2. Our brains **can/can't** tell the difference between different kinds of physical sensations.

3. Our reactions to different physical sensations **are/are not** a result of the type of information our brains give us.

4. If the robot arm of the "tickling machine" touches the hand of the person at the moment he/she pressed the button, it **tickles/doesn't tickle** because our brains make it possible for us to tell the difference between the touch of another person and our own touch.

5. The cerebellum **informs/doesn't inform** us about how much attention we need to give to sensory information we receive.

VOCABULARY

A **Parts of Speech**

Find the words in bold in the reading. Decide if the words are nouns (words that describe people, places, things, qualities, actions, or ideas), verbs (words that describe actions, experiences, or states), or adjectives (words that describe nouns or pronouns). Write the part of speech on the line next to each word.

1. consequences: _____noun_____   6. region: _____

2. unaware: _____   7. distinguish: _____

3. pure: _____   8. unexpected: _____

4. accomplish: _____   9. ignore: _____

5. fool: _____

B Synonyms

Choose a word from the box that is a synonym (word that has the same meaning) as the word in parentheses. Write the word on the line.

accomplish	distinguish	ignore	region
consequences	fooled	pure	

1. You can't tickle yourself because your brain predicts the

   _____ consequences _____ of all your movements, so there is no surprise,
   (outcome)
   and you only feel a light touch instead of a tickle.

2. If our brains only told us that all physical content was

   _____ touch sensation, we wouldn't be able to
   (total)
   _____ a friendly touch from an unfriendly one.
   (tell)

3. The development of the "tickling machine" helped scientists

   _____ their goal, which was to prove why we cannot
   (achieve)
   tickle ourselves.

4. If the robot's touch on the "tickling machine" does not happen

   immediately after the person pushes the button, that person's brain is

   _____, and the person believes someone else
   (tricked)
   touched them.

5. The cerebellum is the _____ of the brain whose name
   (part)
   means "little brain."

A **prefix** is a group of letters added to the beginning of a word that changes the word's meaning. Knowing what prefixes mean can help you understand more as you read.

The Prefix _Un-_

_un-_ = **not**

In adjectives and adverbs, _un-_ is used to show an opposite or negative state:

As we write, we are <u>unaware</u> of the feel of the chair and the texture of our socks. [not aware]

Work with a partner to complete the sentences. Circle the correct answer.

1. I was **aware/unaware** that my teacher walked into the room because I didn't hear her open the classroom door.

2. Our brains are **able/unable** to predict the results of different types of sensory information.

3. Our brains can protect us by letting us know when a sensation is **expected/unexpected**.

4. This is one way our brain helps to keep us **protected/unprotected**.

CRITICAL THINKING

Discuss the ideas with a partner.

1. Find an example of how our brains help us to focus in paragraph 1.

2. Find an example of how our brains help us to protect ourselves in paragraph 3.

3. What fact in the reading did you find most interesting? Why?

Ⓐ Warm-Up

List the ways you think laughter is beneficial. Share your answers with the class.

Ⓑ Reading Strategy

Predicting Type of Text from the Title

Predicting is a very important pre-reading skill. When you **predict**, you make a guess about something based on the information you have. Predicting helps prepare the reader for the reading experience that is to come. The title of a text can often help you predict the type of text. At the same time it helps you to imagine the situation for which the text was written or prepared.

Look at the title of the reading. Do you think the text contains mostly facts or opinions? Discuss your answer with a partner.

Now read the text to find out if your prediction was correct.

Laughter and the Brain

By Eric H. Chudler

1 Laughter . . . it's fun . . . it's funny . . . but why do we do it? What part of the brain is responsible for laughter and **humor**? There are not many answers to these questions because there have not been very many experiments on laughter. Part of the reason for this is that laughter is not a big medical problem.

2 A paper published in the journal *Nature* (vol. 391, page 650, 1998) called "Electric Current Stimulates Laughter" has provided a bit more information about how the brain is involved with laughter. The paper discussed the case of a 16-year-old girl named "A.K." who was having surgery to control seizures[1] **due to** epilepsy.[2] During surgery, the doctors electrically stimulated[3]

(continued on next page)

---

[1] *seizures:* brief periods when someone is unconscious and cannot control the movements of his/her body

[2] *epilepsy:* a medical condition in the brain that can make someone become unconscious or unable to control his/her movements for a short time

[3] *electrically stimulated:* used the power carried by wires to get a muscle or group of muscles to move

A.K.'s cerebral cortex to map her brain.[4] Mapping of the brain is done to determine the function of different brain areas and to make sure that brain tissue that will be removed does not have an important function.

3   The doctors found that A.K. always laughed when they stimulated a small 2 cm by 2 cm area on her left superior frontal gyrus (part of the frontal lobe of the brain). This brain area is part of the supplementary motor area.[5] Each time her brain was stimulated, A.K. laughed and said that something was funny. The thing that she said caused her to laugh was different each time. A.K. laughed first, then **made up** a story that was funny to her. Most people first know what is funny, then they laugh.

4   The authors of the paper believe that the area of the brain that caused laughter in A.K. is part of several different brain areas which are important for:
   - the emotions produced by a funny situation (emotional part of humor)
   - the "**getting it**" part of a joke (cognitive, thinking part of humor)
   - moving the muscles of the face to smile (motor part of humor).

5   The physiological study of laughter has its own name: "gelotology." Research has shown that laughing is more than just a person's voice and movement. Laughter requires the **coordination** of many muscles throughout the body. Laughter also:
   - **increases** blood pressure
   - increases heart rate
   - changes breathing
   - **reduces** levels of certain hormones.[6]
   - provides a **boost** to the immune system.[7]

6   Can laughter improve health? It may be a good way for people to relax because muscle tension is **reduced** after laughing. There are some cases when a good deep laugh may help people with breathing problems. Perhaps laughing can also help heart patients by giving the heart a bit of a workout. Some hospitals even have their own "humor rooms," "**comedy** carts," and clown kids in attempts to speed a patient's recovery and boost **morale**.

---

[4] *map her brain:* to make a visual representation of her brain

[5] *supplementary motor area:* a part of the brain that helps control movement

[6] *hormones:* substances produced by your body that influence its growth, development, and condition

[7] *immune system:* the system by which the body protects itself against disease

COMPREHENSION

A **Main Ideas**

Write the number of the paragraph that matches each main idea from the reading.

1. Paragraph _____ is about how people's health might improve faster from laughter.

2. Paragraph _____ describes different areas of the brain that are responsible for laughter.

3. Paragraph _____ explains that there are not many scientific studies about why we laugh.

4. Paragraph _____ is about surgery done on a teenage girl to control her epileptic seizures.

5. Paragraph _____ is about the physical benefits of laughter.

6. Paragraph _____ explains a discovery the scientists made about the part of our brain that causes laughter.

B **Close Reading**

Complete the sentences by matching a sentence beginning on the left with its ending on the right.

1. In an article called "Electric Current Stimulates Laughter" doctors explained

2. In this reading, humor is divided into three parts:

3. Laughter can

4. Laughter can improve people's health

a. by relaxing muscles.

b. emotional, cognitive (thinking), and motor (muscle movement).

c. that every time they stimulated a small area of their patient's brain, she laughed.

d. change someone's breathing.

VOCABULARY

A Connotations

> Some words have **feelings** connected to them depending on how they are used in a sentence. These feelings, or **connotations**, can be **positive** (good or useful) or **negative** (bad or harmful).

Look at each word. Find it in the reading. Decide whether it has a *Positive* or *Negative* meaning. Check the appropriate box. Discuss your answers with a partner.

	POSITIVE	NEGATIVE
1. humor	☐	☐
2. getting it	☐	☐
3. comedy	☐	☐
4. morale	☐	☐

B Antonyms

Underline the antonym (the word that has the opposite meaning) of the word in bold. Compare your answers with a partner.

1. **humor**	funniness	<u>seriousness</u>	comedy
2. **due to**	because of	as a result of	in addition to
3. **increase**	reduce	raise	improve
4. **boost**	increase	improve	decrease
5. **morale**	insecurity	optimism	self-confidence
6. **get it**	understand	misinterpret	comprehend

C Using the Dictionary

Read the dictionary entry for the phrasal verb *make up*.

> **make (something) up** *phr. v.* **1** to invent a story or explanation to deceive someone **2** to produce a new story, song, game, etc. **3** to work at times when you don't usually work because you have not done enough work at some other time

Read each sentence. Decide which meaning of the verb is being used. Write the number of the appropriate meaning.

_____ **a.** In the "humor rooms" at hospitals, volunteers **make up** funny stories to get patients to laugh.

_____ **b.** When a child asks a question that adults don't know how to answer, they sometimes **make up** an answer just so the child stops asking questions.

_____ **c.** When Mary's husband came home at 11 P.M. and saw she was still **making up** the work . . .

_____ **d.** from when she had been sick, he **made up** a joke to get her to laugh and relax.

> **make (something) of (somebody or something)** *phr. v.* **1** to have a particular opinion about someone or something, or a particular way of understanding something **2 make the most of (something)** to use an opportunity in a way that gives you as much advantage as possible **3 make too much of (something)** to treat a situation as if it is more important than it really is

Read each sentence. Fill in the blank with the appropriate phrasal verb.

a. Do you think the article "Laughter and the Brain" _____ the effects of laughter?

b. Sometimes, humor can be the best way to _____ a difficult situation.

c. At first doctors did not know what to _____ A.K's laughter during the surgical procedure.

NOTE-TAKING: Categorizing

Look at the notes about details from the reading. Decide if each detail is about "laughter" or "the brain" and list each in the correct category.

- a small 2 cm by 2 cm area can be stimulated and cause laughter
- boosts morale
- can be mapped to determine the function of different brain areas
- caused by something funny
- coordinates muscle movements needed to laugh
- helps patients feel more optimistic
- may help breathing problems and heart patients
- may help people recover faster
- more than just a person's voice and movement
- not a medical problem
- reduces muscle tension

LAUGHTER	THE BRAIN

CRITICAL THINKING

Discuss the questions in a small group. Be prepared to share your ideas with the class.

1. In paragraph 3, the doctors found that A.K. laughed when they stimulated a small area of her brain and then she made up a funny story to explain her laughter, which is the opposite of how laughter usually occurs. What did this discovery suggest?

2. How has the study of laughter affected the treatment of patients in some hospitals?

3. Why do you think laughter might help people recover faster?

4. Sitcoms like *Friends* are popular around the world. Why do you think these types of television shows are so popular and attract people of all ages and cultures?

AFTER YOU READ

WRITING ACTIVITY

Choose one of the topics and write a paragraph about it. Use at least five of the words and phrases you studied in the chapter (for a complete list, go to page 146).

1. Do you think "humor rooms" and "comedy carts" would be possible in hospitals in your country? Why or why not?

2. Who is the funniest person you know? What makes them so funny?

DISCUSSION AND WRITING TOPICS

Discuss these topics in a small group. Choose one of them and write a paragraph or two about it. Use the vocabulary from the chapter.

1. The actor Charlie Chaplin said: "A day without laughter is a day wasted." Do you agree with this quote? Give reasons and examples to support your opinion.

2. Comedian Bill Cosby points out: "You can turn painful situations around through laughter. If you can find humor in anything, even poverty, you can survive it." What do you think this quote means? Discuss a time when this was true for you. Give as many details as possible.

VOCABULARY

Nouns	Verbs	Adjectives	Phrases and Idioms
boost	accomplish	pure	get it
comedy	distinguish	unaware*	make up
consequences*	fool	unexpected	tell apart
coordination*	ignore*		
humor	increase	**Preposition**	
morale	reduce	due to	
region*			

* = AWL (Academic Word List) item

SELF-ASSESSMENT

In this chapter you learned to:

○ Scan a text to answer a question in the title

○ Predict the type of text from the title

○ Understand and use the prefix *un-*

○ Determine whether a word has a positive or negative meaning

○ Identify parts of speech

○ Understand and use synonyms and antonyms

○ Use dictionary entries to learn different meanings of a phrasal verb

○ Categorize notes

What can you do well? ✓

What do you need to practice more? ✓

VOCABULARY INDEX

The number following each entry is the page where the word, phrase, or idiom first appears. Words followed by an asterisk (*) are on the Academic Word List (AWL). The AWL is a list of the highest-frequency words found in academic texts.

CREDITS

TEXT CREDITS

Page 3 Sarah Burke, "In the Presence of Animals," *U.S. News & World Report*, February 16, 1992, p. 64. © U.S. News & World Report. Used with permission. All rights reserved; **Page 8** Marianne Mott/National Geographic News. All rights reserved. Reproduced by permission; **Page 18** From CNN.com, February 3, 2011 © 2011 Cable News Network, Inc. All rights reserved. Used by permission and protected by the Copyright Laws of the United States. The printing, copying, redistribution, or retransmission of this Content without express written permission is prohibited; **Page 23** GetSetGrow Editors, "Who Moved My Cheese Review," www.getsetgrow.org, October 1, 2010. Used with permission. All rights reserved; **Page 43** Brittany Karford, "Languages die out, taking history along," *The Daily Universe*, March 16, 2002. All rights reserved. Reproduced by permission; **Page 52** Dan Schorn and Michael Gavshon, "The Elephant Orphanage," *CBS News*. © CBS NEWS ARCHIVES. Reproduced by permission. All rights reserved; **Page 56** Charles Siebert/National Geographic Stock; **Page 65** from WGBH's FRONTLINE A Class Divided website (http://www.pbs.org/wgbh/pages/frontline/shows/divided/etc/synopsis.html) ©1995–2011 WGBH Educational Foundation; **Page 70** Yale University Film Records (RU 760). Manuscripts and Archives, Yale University Library; **Page 93** Susan Krauss Whitbournce, *Psychology Today*, "Fulfillment at Any Age," September 28, 2010; **Page 109** Adapted from Richard Panchyk, *Our Supreme Court*. Chicago: Chicago Review Press; **Page 122** Content © 2012 AOL Inc. Used with permission; **Page 135** Sandra Aamodt and Sam Wang, "Why You Can't Tickle Yourself," *Welcome to Your Brain*. New York: Bloomsbury Publishing. pp 60–61. All rights reserved. Reproduced by permission; **Page 139** Eric H. Chudler, "Laughter and the Brain," http://faculty.washington.edu/chuder/laugh.html, 2008. Used with permission. All rights reserved; **Dictionary entries** From *Longman Dictionary of American English*, New Edition, © 2004 Copyright © Pearson Education. All rights reserved. Reproduced by permission.

PHOTO CREDITS

Page 1 Galina Barskaya/Fotolia; **p. 2** byrdyak/Fotolia; **p. 3** David Grossman/Alamy; **p. 4** Ivonne Wierink/Fotolia; **p. 7** lightpoet/Fotolia; **p. 8** Ingo Wagner/dpa/picture-alliance/Newscom; **p. 16** Mikael Damkier/Fotolia; **p. 17** Sharon Day/Fotolia; **p. 18** Courtesy of Gridiron Heroes Spinal Cord Injury Foundation; **p. 30** freshidea/Fotolia; **p. 32** dbimages/Alamy; **p. 34** sciencephotos/Alamy; **p. 35** AP Images/USMC via National Archives; **p. 41** domdeen/Fotolia; **p. 42** steve bly/Alamy; **p. 44** DK Images; **p. 46** John Brown/Alamy; **p. 50** javarman/Fotolia; **p. 52** Peter Barritt/Alamy; **p. 55** Digitalpress/Fotolia; **p. 56** Kitch Bain/Fotolia; **p. 60** amrishwad/Fotolia; **p. 63** mangostock/Fotolia; **p. 64** Colin Bootman/The Bridgeman Art Library/Getty Images; **p. 65** Courtesy of Elliott, Jane; **p. 77** (top) age fotostock/Robert Harding, (bottom) maurice joseph/Alamy; **p. 78** AP Images/Chris Gardner; **p. 79** david pearson/Alamy; **p. 85** eye ubiquitous/Robert Harding; **p. 91** Bob Jenkin/Alamy; **p. 93** SHOUT/Alamy; **p. 97** Radius Images/Alamy; **p. 99** New York Daily News Archive/Getty Images; **p. 100** Robert Kalfus/Splash News/Newscom; **p. 106** (top) bbourdages/Fotolia, (middle) Sandra Manske/Fotolia, (bottom) Gary Blakeley/Fotolia; **p. 109** Henryk Sadura/Shutterstock; **p. 113** (left) Handout/MCT/Newscom, (right) Rapport Press/Newscom; **p. 116** xy/Fotolia; **p. 120** Ronald Karpilo/Alamy; **p. 121** Michelle Chaplow/Alamy; **p. 122** Francis DEMANGE/Getty Images; **p. 126** AP Images/ Hermann J. Knippertz; **p. 127** AP Images/ Hermann J. Knippertz; **p. 131** auremar/Fotolia; **p. 133** Athanasia Nomikou/Fotolia; **p. 135** Susan Stevenson/Fotolia; **p. 139** Edyta Pawlowska/Fotolia.

ILLUSTRATION CREDITS

Page 107 TSI Graphics